Reading Advantage 3

Second Edition

Casey Malarcher

THOMSON

HEINLE

Australia · Canada · Mexico · Singapore · Spain · United Kingdom · United States

THOMSON

HEINLE

Reading Advantage, Second Edition, **Student Book 3**

Casey Malarcher

Publisher, Global ELT: Christopher Wenger
Editorial Manager: Sean Bermingham
Development Editor: Derek Mackrell
Production Editor: Tan Jin Hock
ELT Directors: John Lowe (Asia), Jim Goldstone (Latin America—ELT), Francisco Lozano (Latin America—Academic and Training, ELT)

Director of Marketing, ESL/ELT: Amy Mabley
Marketing Manager: Ian Martin
Interior/Cover Design: Christopher Hanzie, TYA Inc.
Composition: Stella Tan and Ronn Lee, TYA Inc.
Cover Images: PhotoDisc, Inc.
Printer: Seng Lee Press

Printed in Singapore
1 2 3 4 5 6 7 8 9 10   07 06 05 04 03

For permission to use material from this text or product, contact us in the United States:
Tel   1-800-730-2214
Fax   1-800-730-2215
Web   www.thomsonrights.com

For more information, contact Heinle, 25 Thomson Place, Boston, Massachusetts 02210 USA, or you can visit our Internet site at http://www.heinle.com

ISBN 1-4130-0116-5

Credits

Unless otherwise stated, all photos are from PhotoDisc, Inc. Digital Imagery © copyright 2003 PhotoDisc, Inc. Photos on pages 27 and 49 are the exclusive property of Heinle. Photos from other sources: pages 5, 43, 57, and 79: Index Stock; pages 17, 21, 31, 39, and 83: Reuters/Landov; page 61: Kyodo/Landov; page 65: Bloomberg News/Landov; page 71: Bettmann/CORBIS; page 87: Reuters NewMedia Inc./CORBIS

Dictionary definitions are adapted from Heinle's *Newbury House Dictionary of American English*, © 2002, Monroe Allen Publishers, Inc. Barbie® (Unit 9) is a registered trademark of Mattel, Inc. Botox® (Unit 9) is a registered trademark of Allergan Corporation.
Sources of information: http://en.wikipedia.org/wiki/Spider and http://www.nexiabiotech.com/pdf/pr/2002-01-17%20-%20Science%20Paper%20-%20English.pdf (Unit 1); http://www.pbs.org/wgbh/nova/pyramid/explore/sphinx.html and http://en.wikipedia.org/wiki/Sphinx (Unit 2); http://dear_raed.blogspot.com/ and http://www.marginwalker.org/1imc/conference.html (Unit 3); http://entertainment.msn.com/news/article.aspx?news =131054, http://www.wunderland.com/WTS/Andy/Leftovers/ForAllMankind.html, and http://www.theage.com.au/articles/2003/06/11/1055220651907.html (Unit 4); *Los Angeles Times*, July 23, 2003, "In Cycling, Winning with Honor Means Everything" (Unit 5); http://www.guardian.co.uk/uk_news/story/0,3604,1034645,00.html (Review 1–5); http://www.left-handersday.com/ and http://duke.usask.ca/~elias/left/ (Unit 6); http://news.bbc.co.uk/cbbcnews/hi/

tv_film/newsid_2806000/2806381.stm and http://www.canoe.ca/JamMoviesArtistsL/lopez_jennifer.html (Unit 7); http://www.guardian.co.uk/g2/story/0,3604,856700,00.html and http://www.plasticsurgery.org/public_education/profile_andrew.cfm (Unit 9); http://people.hofstra.edu/geotrans/eng/ch5en/appl5en/ch5a1en.html, http://www.oilspill.state.ak.us/facts/bibliographies.html, and http://www.itopf.com/stats.html (Unit 10); http://www.american.edu/ted/minamata.htm and http://www.unu.edu/unupress/unupbooks/uu35ie/uu35ie0c.htm (Review 6–10); http://www.korcula.net/mpolo/mpolo5.htm, http://en.wikipedia.org/wiki/Mail, and http://inventors.about.com/library/inventors/blmail.htm (Unit 11); http://www.jsonline.com/news/metro/may03/142451.asp and Deyo, Yaacov & Deyo, Sue (2002) *Speed Dating: The Smarter, Faster Way to Lasting Love*, Harper Resource (Unit 12); http://www.aboutfamouspeople.com/article1231.html and http://www.prairieghosts.com/winchester.html (Unit 13); http://sportsillustrated.cnn.com/inside_game/john_donovan/news/2003/07/11/international_players/ and http://reds.enquirer.com/2003/02/24/wwwred4c24.html (Unit 14); *The Guinness Book of World Records 1998,* Bantam Books (Unit 15); http://www.sealandgov.com (Review 11–15); http://www.columbia.edu/~brennan/abandoned/cityirt.html and http://www.nycsubway.org/irt/eastside/irt-eastside-cityhall.html (Unit 16); http://www.nps.gov/whsa/ (Unit 18); Redding, Stan & Abagnale, Frank (2000) *Catch Me If You Can: The True Story of a Real Fake,* Broadway Books (Unit 19); http://www.guardian.co.uk/arts/saatchi/page/0,13010,928758,00.html (Unit 20); http://en.wikipedia.org/wiki/Ninja (Review 16–20)

Contents

Preface

Welcome to *Reading Advantage Book 3*! In this book, you will find readings and exercises to help build your English vocabulary and reading skills. Each of the units in this book is divided into seven parts. These parts should be studied together to help you develop reading skills, as well as review new vocabulary and reinforce vocabulary presented in other units.

Before You Read

This part of each unit presents questions for you to think about before you read the passage. The questions focus on knowledge you may already have on the subject of the passage, as well as questions which will be answered in the reading. You should discuss (or write) the answers to these questions before reading.

Target Vocabulary

In this section, you are introduced to words from the reading that you may not know. You should be able to match the words with the simple definitions provided. After studying these words, continue with the reading.

Reading Passage

Each reading passage in Book 3 is around 470 words in length. First read this passage alone silently. At the end of each passage, the word count for the readings is shown, with a space to record your reading time for the passage. By keeping track of your reading times, using the chart inside the back cover of this book, you will be able to see the improvement in your reading speeds over the course. Each reading is recorded on the audio cassette/CD; after reading through silently, listen to the passage spoken by a native English speaker.

Reading Comprehension

This section is a series of multiple-choice questions about the passage. You are encouraged to look back at the reading in order to check your answers to these questions. The questions cover important reading skills, such as understanding the main idea, scanning for details, and reading for inference.

Idioms

This section highlights three idioms from the reading passage. The meaning of these idioms and examples of how they may be used are presented.

Vocabulary Reinforcement

This section is divided into two parts. Section A has eight multiple-choice sentences for vocabulary and idiom practice. Section B presents a cloze passage with missing words to complete using vocabulary items from the box. Vocabulary and idioms tested in this section have been selected from the present unit, as well as earlier units in the book.

What Do You Think?

In this section, you are encouraged to think further about what you have read and communicate your own ideas and feelings about the topics presented. Answers to these questions can be used as a writing activity.

There are also four review units in this book—one after every five units. These will help you to check what you have learned.

I hope you enjoy using *Reading Advantage*!

Casey Malarcher

Spiders

Before You Read

Answer the following questions.

1. Are spiders popular as pets in your country? Why or why not?

   _____

   _____

2. Are you, or is anyone you know, scared of spiders?

   _____

   _____

3. Do you think spiders have any uses?

   _____

   _____

Target Vocabulary

Match each word with the best meaning.

1. _____ artificial	**a.**	from a particular area
2. _____ benefit	**b.**	the army, air force, and navy
3. _____ environment	**c.**	made by humans; not made naturally
4. _____ military	**d.**	(verb) to receive a positive result; (noun) a positive result
5. _____ native (to)	**e.**	the possibility of something
6. _____ potential	**f.**	large or important
7. _____ reputation	**g.**	opinion about how good something is
8. _____ significant	**h.**	a grouping of living things
9. _____ species	**i.**	the air, land, water, and surroundings that people, plants, and animals live in
10. _____ fund	**j.**	(verb) to provide money for a purpose; (noun) a sum of money for a purpose

There are more than 37,000 known **species** of spiders in the world in a wide variety of shapes and sizes. The largest spiders in the world live in the rain forests of South America and are known by the people who live there as the "bird-eating spiders." These spiders can grow up to 28 centimeters in length—about the size
5 of a dinner plate, and, as their name suggests, have been known to eat small birds. In comparison, the smallest species of spider in the world is **native** to Western Samoa. These tiny spiders are less than half a millimeter long—about the size of a period on this page—and live in plants that grow on mountain rocks.

Some people like to keep spiders as pets, particularly tarantulas, which are native
10 to North America and can live for up to twenty-five years. Most people, on the other hand, don't like touching spiders, and a **significant** number of people are afraid of them, mainly because of their poison. However, despite their bad **reputation**, only thirty of the 37,000 known species of spiders are deadly to humans. Spiders actually provide **benefits** to humans, by catching and eating
15 harmful insects such as flies and mosquitoes.

The main thing that makes spiders different from other animals is that they spin webs to catch the small insects they feed on. The unique silk of a spider's web is produced by special organs found in the lower part of the spider's body. It is light, elastic, and strong—spider web is five times stronger than steel. Additionally, it is
20 completely biodegradable.[1] This means that the web will completely decompose[2] and eventually return to nature over time—making it perfect for uses such as making fishing nets. Some people have tried to raise spiders commercially in order to collect the silk these spiders produce, but no one has ever really managed to make a go of it. One reason why these businesses never stand a chance is because
25 it takes 670,000 spiders to produce half a kilogram of silk, and all of these spiders need living insects for their food. In addition, spiders are usually solitary[3] animals, and need to be kept alone.

One Canadian company may have found a solution to making **artificial** spider web. In 2002, they announced that they had used genetically modified goats to
30 produce milk that contains the chemicals used to make spider web. The company, which is **funded** by the U.S. army, hopes that in the long run it will be able to make large quantities of very light, very strong fiber for **military** and medical uses. Additionally, because the manufacture of the artificial web is based on goat's milk and water, the industry **potentially** would be non-polluting and
35 **environmentally** friendly.

 _____ **minutes** _____ **seconds** (461 words)

---

[1] **biodegradable** breaks down completely, and can be thrown away without causing pollution
[2] **decompose** decay and go into the ground over time, e.g., dead leaves or fruit
[3] **solitary** living alone rather than in groups

Reading Comprehension

Circle the letter of the best answer.

1. What is the best title for this passage?

   a. The Spider—An Amazing Animal

   b. Why People Hate Spiders

   c. The World's Largest Spider

   d. How Spider Webs Are Made

2. According to this passage, spiders are . . .

   a. deadly and useless.

   b. unpopular but beneficial.

   c. harmful but popular.

   d. uncommon and not significant.

3. Spider web and steel are both _____.

   a. strong

   b. light

   c. biodegradable

   d. elastic

4. What characteristic of spider web would make fishing nets made from it environmentally friendly?

   a. strength

   b. elasticity

   c. lightness

   d. biodegradability

5. What sentence is NOT true about the Canadian researchers?

   a. They have produced goats that can spin webs.

   b. They receive money from the American army.

   c. Their technique for producing webs causes little pollution.

   d. They are able to produce web without using spiders.

Idioms

Find each idiom in the story.

1. **make a go of something**—*have success with something*
   - I thought his business would fail, but he's really **making a go of** it.
   - Kylie wanted to **make a go of** her marriage, but her husband wanted a divorce.

2. **stand a chance**—*likely to achieve something*
   - I'd love it if my team won, but I don't think they **stand a chance**.
   - I'll have to study hard to **stand a chance** of passing that exam.

3. **as (the) name suggests**—*as defined by the name*
   - Big Jim, **as his name suggests**, is a large man.
   - The Man-Eating Tiger of Borneo, **as its name suggests**, killed and ate a number of people.

Vocabulary Reinforcement

A. Circle the letter of the word or phrase that best completes the sentence.

1. The inventor had a hard time finding someone with money to _____ his new invention.

    a. suggest   **b.** fund   **c.** stand a chance of   **d.** benefit

2. Many scientists don't feel comfortable doing research for _____ purposes.

    a. military   **b.** beneficial   **c.** artificial   **d.** comparative

3. I think you can trust him; he has a good _____.

    a. benefit   **b.** species   **c.** organ   **d.** reputation

4. Kangaroos are _____ Australia.

    a. beneficial for   **b.** native to   **c.** as the name suggests   **d.** deadly to

5. Andrea has a terrible voice. She doesn't _____ of winning the singing contest.

    a. make a go   **b.** stand a chance   **c.** have a reputation   **d.** find a solution

6. Green tree frogs, _____, live in trees.

    a. eventually   **b.** even though   **c.** as the name suggests   **d.** unfortunately

7. To me, sugar tastes better than _____ sweeteners.

    a. species   **b.** artificial   **c.** useful   **d.** significant

8. Often, historical events that didn't seem _____ at the time end up being very important later on.

    a. delicious   **b.** potential   **c.** artificial   **d.** significant

B. Complete the passage with items from the box. One item is extra.

artificial   benefit   environment   make a go of   potentially   species   reputations

The thousands of different (1)_____ of spiders range from the size of dinner plates to smaller than a period. Spiders are unique because they spin webs of silk, and some people think spider silk is (2)_____ useful for humans. Spider web silk is very strong and is biodegradable, so it is good for the (3)_____. No modern businesses have been able to (4)_____ spider farming, but one company claims to have found a way to produce the chemicals to make (5)_____ web silk through goat's milk. If this company is successful, the new silk could (6)_____ people in many ways.

What Do You Think?

1. What other animals have a bad reputation? Do they deserve their unpopularity?

2. What do you think about genetically modified animals and plants? Do you think genetic modification is a good idea?

The Sphinx

Before You Read

Answer the following questions.

1. What do you know about the monument in the picture? _____

2. Do you know any other Egyptian monuments? _____

3. What are some famous monuments in your country? _____

Target Vocabulary

Match each word with the best meaning.

1. _____ archaeologist   **a.** to make something look like it did when it was new

2. _____ cane   **b.** easy to see

3. _____ crawl   **c.** a stick made of wood or metal used to help a person walk

4. _____ monument   **d.** to move slowly and close to the ground

5. _____ restore   **e.** a person, animal, or thing made from wood, stone, or metal

6. _____ riddle   **f.** to show great respect for

7. _____ statue   **g.** a question that requires cleverness to answer

8. _____ strangle   **h.** to kill someone by squeezing their neck so they can't breathe

9. _____ visible   **i.** a sculpture or building built in memory of a person or historical event

10. _____ worship   **j.** a person who studies historical people and cultures by looking at old things

9

For any tourist visiting Egypt, there are two things that everyone must see. The first is the 137-meter-high Great Pyramid of Giza,[1] the largest of all the pyramids in Egypt. The second is the Great Sphinx of Giza, a sculpture with the body of a lion and the head of a man, which stands 20 meters tall and 73 meters long.

5 The origin of the Great Sphinx of Giza goes back 5,000 years. Although many sphinx sculptures have been found over the years, researchers believe that the Great Sphinx which guards the pyramids in Giza was actually the first one to be made (around 2600–2500 B.C.). The head of the Sphinx represents Khafre, the Pharaoh[2] who ruled Egypt at that time.

10 About two thousand years later, around 570 B.C., sand had covered all but the head of the Great Sphinx. The people living in the area had forgotten the history of the **statue**, so they imagined that the head represented the sun god Ra and began **worshiping** it. The son of Pharaoh Amenhotep II heard the head speak to him in a dream. The Sphinx's head made him promise to clear the sand from the 15 statue's body. The son, Thutmose, kept his word and did what he was told in the dream. He also built walls around the statue to prevent the sand from covering it again. After all of the sand was cleared away, Thutmose made a large stone tablet[3] that told the story of his dream. He placed this tablet between the two front feet of the Sphinx, where it stands to this day.

20 For hundreds of years, the Sphinx attracted people both as a religious **monument** and as a work of art. But eventually, the desert sand once again covered the Sphinx, leaving only the head **visible**. It was not until the 1800s that **archaeologists** began clearing the sand from the statue and began researching the long history of the Sphinx. At last, in the 1920s, all of the sand was finally 25 cleared away and **restoration** work, which continues to this day, was begun.

The name "sphinx" comes from an ancient Greek word, meaning "**strangler**." According to Greek legend, the Sphinx was a demon[4] with the body of a winged lion, and the head of a woman. She sat beside a road, and asked all people who passed her a **riddle**: "Which animal in the morning goes on four feet, at noon on 30 two, and on three in the evening?" She strangled anyone who couldn't make sense of the question. The riddle was finally solved by the Greek king, Oedipus. The answer was man, who **crawls** on hands and knees as a baby, then walks on two feet as an adult, and finally walks with a **cane** in old age. The Sphinx then threw herself from her high rock and died.

_____ **minutes** _____ **seconds** (475 words)

---

[1] **Giza** a town in Egypt, now part of Cairo
[2] **Pharaoh** the title of the kings of ancient Egypt
[3] **tablet** a flat piece of clay or stone with writing on it
[4] **demon** an evil creature; a devil

Reading Comprehension

Circle the letter of the best answer.

1. What is this passage mainly about?
   - **a.** how the Great Sphinx is being restored
   - **b.** the history of the Great Sphinx
   - **c.** the history of the Egyptian Pharaohs
   - **d.** the monuments of Egypt

2. Which statement about the Great Sphinx is true?
   - **a.** It is the only sphinx in the world.
   - **b.** It is the largest monument in Egypt.
   - **c.** It was built by the ancient Greeks.
   - **d.** It has been covered by sand at least twice.

3. The Great Sphinx was built as a monument to who?
   - **a.** Khafre
   - **b.** Amenhotep II
   - **c.** Ra
   - **d.** Oedipus

4. What sentence about the Great Sphinx is NOT true?
   - **a.** It is no longer covered by sand.
   - **b.** People today believe that it represents the sun god Ra.
   - **c.** It is still being restored.
   - **d.** You can still see a tablet in front of it.

5. According to legend, how did the Sphinx die?
   - **a.** Oedipus killed her.
   - **b.** She died of old age.
   - **c.** She killed herself.
   - **d.** She was strangled.

Idioms

Find each idiom in the story.

1. **to this day**—*until and including today*
   - She left her country when she was sixteen and **to this day** has never been back.
   - The mystery of Jim Thomson's disappearance is unsolved **to this day**.

2. **keep one's word**—*do what you say you will do*
   - You can really trust Junichi. He always **keeps his word**.
   - I didn't think she'd remember her promise, but she **kept her word**.

3. **make sense (of)**—*able to be understood; succeed in understanding*
   - Can you help me with this question? I can't **make sense of** it.
   - No one could understand why he killed himself. It just didn't **make sense**.

Vocabulary Reinforcement

A. Circle the letter of the word or phrase that best completes the sentence.

1. Before babies can walk, they learn to _____.

   a. strangle   **b.** worship   **c.** crawl   **d.** restore

2. Which of these would be most useful in helping an elderly person walk?

   a. a statue   **b.** a cane   **c.** a riddle   **d.** an archaeologist

3. To celebrate the town's anniversary, they funded a _____ of the founder.

   a. statue   **b.** species   **c.** pyramid   **d.** tablet

4. To be thought of as honest, you should always _____.

   a. make sense   **b.** make a go of it   **c.** clear away   **d.** keep your word

5. My grandfather had a bicycle accident in 1973 and _____ hasn't been on a bike again.

   a. as the name suggests   **b.** in the long run   **c.** to this day   **d.** these days

6. "Why did the chicken cross the road?" is a very old _____.

   a. riddle   **b.** monument   **c.** restoration   **d.** demon

7. That old house will need to be _____ before people can live in it again.

   a. ruled   **b.** restored   **c.** funded   **d.** worshiped

8. Road signs are usually painted in bright colors to make them more _____.

   a. artificial   **b.** visible   **c.** potential   **d.** deadly

B. Complete the passage with items from the box. One item is extra.

archaeologists	make sense	monument	restored	visible	worship	strangled

The Sphinx is a very famous (1)_____ in Egypt that almost every tourist there goes to see. According to (2)_____, the Great Sphinx of Giza was probably the first sphinx made. Over thousands of years, sand covered the Sphinx until only the head was (3)_____. People forgot that the head represented a Pharaoh, and they began to (4)_____ the Sphinx as Ra, the sun god. In fact, the name "sphinx" is not Egyptian, but from the Greek word meaning "strangler." According to legend, the Sphinx (5)_____ and killed anyone who could not (6)_____ of her riddle.

What Do You Think?

1. Are there any monuments or buildings in your country that should be (or have been) restored?

2. What riddles do you know?

Blogging

Before You Read

Answer the following questions.

1. Have you ever kept a diary? For how long? _____

2. How often do you use the Internet? What do you use it for? _____

3. Look at the title of this unit, and the picture above.
   What do you think this unit is about? _____

Target Vocabulary

Match each word with the best meaning.

1. _____ ally   **a.** a professional meeting, usually at a big hotel

2. _____ ban   **b.** a partner

3. _____ conference   **c.** stop; not allow

4. _____ enable   **d.** an event or happening, usually bad

5. _____ incident   **e.** television, radio, newspapers, and magazines

6. _____ media   **f.** happening at frequent periods

7. _____ regular   **g.** the place where something (often information) comes from

8. _____ shock   **h.** particular; not general

9. _____ source   **i.** to make possible for someone

10. _____ specific   **j.** something unexpected that threatens one's comfort and well-being

When important events are happening around the world, most people turn to traditional **media sources**, such as CNN and BBC,[1] for their news. However, during the invasion of Iraq by the United States and its **allies** in early 2003, a significant number of people followed the war from the point of view of an anonymous[2] Iraqi
5   citizen who called himself "Salam Pax" (*salam* means "peace" in Arabic, and *pax* means "peace" in Latin).

Salam Pax wrote a diary about everyday life in Baghdad during the war, and posted it on his web site. Pax's online diary was a kind of web site known as a "blog." Blogs, short for "web-logs," are online diaries, usually kept by individuals,
10   but sometimes by companies and other groups of people. They are the fastest growing type of web site on the Internet. In 2003, there were estimated to be several hundred thousand blogs on the Internet, and the number was growing by tens of thousands a month.

A blog differs from a traditional web site in several ways. Most importantly, it is
15   updated much more **regularly**. Many blogs are updated every day, and some are updated several times a day. Also, most blogs use special software or web sites which are **specifically** aimed at bloggers, so you don't need to be a computer expert to create your own blog. This means that ordinary people who may find computers difficult to use can easily set up and start writing their own blog. In 2003, the
20   Internet company AOL[3] introduced their own blogging service, **enabling** its 35 million members to quickly and easily start blogging.

There are many different kinds of blogs. The most popular type is an online diary of links, where the blog writer surfs the Internet and then posts links to sites or news articles that they find interesting, with a few comments about each one. Other
25   types are personal diaries, where the writer talks about their life and feelings. Sometimes these blogs can be very personal.

There is another kind of blogging, called "moblogging," short for "mobile blogging." Mobloggers use mobile phones with cameras to take photos, which are posted instantly to the Internet. In 2003, the first international mobloggers
30   **conference** was held in Tokyo. The use of mobile phones in this way made the headlines in Singapore when a high school student posted on the Internet a movie he had taken of a teacher shouting at another student, and tearing up the student's homework. Many people were **shocked** by the student posting a video of the **incident** on the Internet, and wanted phones with cameras to be **banned** from
35   schools.

Many people think that as blogs become more common, news reporting will rely less on big media companies, and more on ordinary people posting news to the Internet. They think that then the news will be less like a lecture, and more like a conversation, where anyone can join in.

_____ **minutes** _____ **seconds** (489 words)

---

[1] **CNN, BBC** Cable News Network, British Broadcasting Corporation
[2] **anonymous** not named; unknown
[3] **AOL** America Online

Reading Comprehension

Circle the letter of the best answer.

1. What is this passage mainly about?

   a. the history of the Internet

   b. the war in Iraq

   c. new types of media

   d. the increase in popularity of computers

2. Which statement about Salam Pax is true?

   a. He worked for CNN.

   b. He lived in an ally country.

   c. Salam Pax is not his real name.

   d. He used a mobile phone for his blog.

3. To start your own blog, what do you need most?

   a. special software

   b. an AOL account

   c. an interesting point of view

   d. access to the Internet

4. What is the most significant difference between blogs and traditional web sites?

   a. Blogs are updated much more often.

   b. Blogs use special software.

   c. Blogs contain links to other web sites.

   d. Blogs contain personal information.

5. According to the passage, which statement about the future is most likely? In the future, . . .

   a. everyone will have a blog.

   b. large media companies will be unnecessary.

   c. people will be able to learn the news from alternative points of view.

   d. blogging technology will be banned.

Idioms

Find each idiom in the story.

1. **find (something + adjective)**—*think that something is (adjective)*
   * I don't know why people think math is difficult. I **find it easy**.
   * Since her baby was born, Nicole **finds it hard** to get time to meet her friends.

2. **make (the) headlines**—*become news*
   * The terrorist attack **made headlines** around the world.
   * The celebrity divorce **made the headlines**.

3. **point of view**—*opinions or feelings one has about something*
   * She always disagrees with me. She just can't see my **point of view**.
   * His **point of view** just doesn't make sense.

Vocabulary Reinforcement

A. Circle the letter of the word or phrase that best matches the word in *italics*.

1. Archaeologists from all over the world came to the *conference*.
   a. party   **b.** meeting   **c.** incident   **d.** monument

2. The two countries were strong *allies*.
   a. competitors   **b.** enemies   **c.** militaries   **d.** partners

3. The *incident* was big news all over the world.
   a. event   **b.** discovery   **c.** decision   **d.** announcement

4. Paulo *regularly* exercises at the gym.
   a. rarely   **b.** sometimes   **c.** often   **d.** never

5. The aim of the new law is to *enable* people to change jobs easily.
   a. stop   **b.** encourage   **c.** discourage   **d.** allow

6. The newspaper article was quite *specific* about the government's problems.
   a. particular   **b.** general   **c.** honest   **d.** limited

7. Smoking is *banned* in the garden.
   a. allowed   **b.** not allowed   **c.** encouraged   **d.** discouraged

8. The Prime Minister's assistant was the *source* of the information.
   a. inventor   **b.** researcher   **c.** announcer   **d.** provider

B. Complete the passage with items from the box. One item is extra.

| banned   found it useful   media   point of view   shocked   source   made the headlines |

When major events happen in the world today, people now have a new way to learn about them in addition to traditional forms of (1)_____. For example, during the war in Iraq in 2003, one blog in particular (2)_____. It was read by many people as a (3)_____ of information on daily life in Baghdad, from the (4)_____ of an Iraqi citizen. Some people have also begun to keep moblogs using mobile phones with cameras in them. However, some people were (5)_____ when one student used his phone to take pictures of a teacher yelling at a student. Some people think such cameras should be (6)_____ from places like schools.

What Do You Think?

1. Do you, or does anyone you know, have a web site? If so, what is it like?
2. If you had a blog, what kind of things would you write about?

Blockbuster Movies

Before You Read

Answer the following questions.

1. What do you know about the actor above?
   What do you think of his movies? _____

2. Do you prefer big-budget movies
   or smaller independent films? _____

3. How much do you think the average
   Hollywood film costs to make? _____

Target Vocabulary

Match each word with the best meaning.

1. _____ budget   **a.** a plan of expected income and expenses over time

2. _____ expect   **b.** poor; modest

3. _____ humble   **c.** well-known or famous for something bad

4. _____ merchandising   **d.** a group of similar things or events

5. _____ minimum   **e.** wonderful; exciting

6. _____ notorious   **f.** need someone or something in order to work or live well

7. _____ rely (on)   **g.** the smallest amount (opposite: maximum—the largest amount)

8. _____ series   **h.** believe something will happen; believe you should have
                                    something
9. _____ spectacular

10. _____ studio   **i.** a company that produces movies; a place where movies
                                    are made

                                   j. toys or clothes made in order to promote something,
                                   e.g., a film, sports team

17

Movies are probably the most popular form of entertainment today. Today's full-length movies began with short motion pictures[1] developed in France in the late 1800s by the Lumière brothers.[2] However, the world's first full-length film, *The Story of the Kelly Gang*, came from Australia. This silent film, which showed the
5   life of the **notorious** criminal Ned Kelly,[3] opened at the Melbourne Town Hall on December 26, 1906. It was over an hour long.

The film industry has come a long way from its **humble** beginning, and today millions of dollars are spent producing and advertising movies. Some of the most expensive movies ever produced include *Terminator 3: Rise of the Machines*
10 (US$175 million), *Titanic* ($200 million), and the *Lord of the Rings* trilogy ($300 million—about $100 million a film). In comparison, the most expensive Bollywood film ever made, *Devdas*, cost only $10 million to make.

However, when you compare the cost of an older movie with the value of money at the time it was made, *Cleopatra* remains the most expensive movie ever made.
15 Elizabeth Taylor played Cleopatra in this film made in 1963. One of the reasons why this movie cost so much money was because Ms. Taylor had 65 different (and very expensive) costumes in the movie! This movie, if made today, would cost a **minimum** of $275 million to shoot.

Some people, however, think that one film beats this record. *For All Mankind*, a
20 documentary about NASA's[4] nine Apollo space missions, was produced from film taken by NASA aboard its spaceships over several years. If the cost of the spaceships is taken into account, the film cost billions of dollars to make!

The average **budget** of most Hollywood movies produced in the 1990s was over $50 million, and movie budgets are still continuing to climb. Often, the movie
25 itself cannot make enough money from ticket sales alone to cover the cost of production, and the **studio relies** on **merchandising** and selling products related to the movie to help make up for poor box office[5] sales. For example, the film *Star Wars*, which was a huge success in terms of box office sales (it made $500 million at the box office), has gone on to make more than $2.5 billion after its release
30 from toys and other merchandising connected to the *Star Wars* **series**.

The problem that Hollywood studios are finding is that as film budgets increase, audiences **expect** more and more **spectacular** special effects—all of which cost increasing amounts of money. "You have to drive the audience into the theater, and they won't be driven into the theater unless you can show them something
35 they haven't seen before," says Joel Silver, the producer of the three *Matrix* films. "You have to wow them." With audiences taking expensive special effects for granted, it seems that for the time being, big budget films are here to stay.

_____ **minutes** _____ **seconds** (480 words)

---

[1] **motion pictures** films, moving pictures, movies
[2] **Lumière brothers** Auguste (1862–1954) and Louis (1864–1948)
[3] **Ned Kelly (1854?–1880)** Australia's most famous historical criminal
[4] **NASA** National Aeronautics and Space Administration
[5] **box office** cinema ticket sales office

Reading Comprehension

Circle the letter of the best answer.

1. What was the subject of the first full-length film?

   a. the Lumière brothers

   b. a thief

   c. a famous Australian building

   d. France in the 1800s

2. Which is true in comparing Hollywood and Bollywood movies?

   a. Bollywood movies are much cheaper.

   b. Hollywood films are much cheaper.

   c. Their movies cost about the same to make.

   d. The passage doesn't say.

3. Why was *For All Mankind* so expensive to make?

   a. The rockets in the film were very expensive to make.

   b. NASA needed to train astronauts to act.

   c. The movie included many famous actors.

   d. The special effects were very expensive.

4. What can be assumed about the average cost of producing a Hollywood movie today?

   a. It is less than $50 million.

   b. It is about $50 million.

   c. It is higher than $50 million.

   d. The cost can't be assumed from the reading.

5. How did *Star Wars* continue to make money after it stopped being shown in cinemas?

   a. by selling items related to the movie

   b. by changing the story

   c. by advertising

   d. by reducing its budget

Idioms

Find each idiom in the story.

1. **take (something) into account**—*consider something when thinking about a situation*
   - If you **take** the cost of postage **into account**, you don't save much money by buying books over the Internet.
   - The thief's long criminal history was **taken into account** and she was sent to prison for a long time.

2. **make up for**—*replace or pay for something that is lost, broken, or missing*
   - Sylvia stayed late at work to **make up for** arriving late.
   - Sebastian bought his girlfriend flowers to **make up for** forgetting her birthday.

3. **take (something) for granted**—*believe something is true or normal without thinking about it*
   - Most waiters in the United States **take** it **for granted** that they will get a tip at the end of the meal.
   - Many husbands and wives start to **take** their partner **for granted** after a few years of marriage.

Vocabulary Reinforcement

A. Circle the letter of the word or phrase that best completes the sentence.

1. The designer of *Hello Kitty* has made a lot of money from _____.
   a. merchandising   b. budgets   c. series   d. studios

2. Jack the Ripper was _____ for murdering many people in the nineteenth century.
   a. spectacular   b. popular   c. notorious   d. specific

3. There are three books (and movies) in the *Lord of the Rings* _____.
   a. species   b. source   c. account   d. series

4. I put on so much weight on my vacation that I need to go to the gym every day to _____.
   a. make up for it   b. make sense of it   c. take it into account   d. take it for granted

5. Naoko is new at her job, and really _____ her manager to help her.
   a. crawls on   b. relies on   c. worships   d. budgets

6. That elevator can take a _____ of twelve people.
   a. maximum   b. minimum   c. ban   d. conference

7. That baseball team wins so often that their fans _____ that they will win.
   a. make up for it   b. take it into account c. take it for granted   d. stand a chance

8. When deciding a new worker's salary, most employers _____ an applicant's experience.
   a. take for granted   b. take into account   c. make up for   d. rely on

B. Complete the passage with items from the box. One item is extra.

budgets   expect   humble   take into account   studios   merchandising   spectacular

Today's modern movie industry had its (1)_____ beginning with the silent
Australian movie *The Story of the Kelly Gang*. Since that time, both the popularity and
(2)_____ of movies have grown an incredible amount. By far, (3)_____
in the United States spend the most, with the average movie in the 1990s costing over $50
million. Today the cost is even higher because people (4)_____ more and more
(5)_____ special effects. Many films today have to rely on (6)_____ to
make back the cost of producing the film.

What Do You Think?

1. Do you agree with Joel Silver? Do movies have to wow the audience with special effects
   to be good?

2. Why do you think action films are so popular?

The Tour de France

Before You Read

Answer the following questions.

1. Do you like cycling? How popular is cycling in your country?

   _____

   _____

2. What long-distance sporting events are popular in your country?

   _____

   _____

3. What do you know about the Tour de France?

   _____

   _____

Target Vocabulary

Match each word with the best meaning.

1. _____ alien	**a.** including everything; total
2. _____ clockwise	**b.** a path along which one travels
3. _____ consist of	**c.** to be made up of
4. _____ cycle	**d.** ride a bicycle
5. _____ dot	**e.** in the direction that the hands of a clock move
6. _____ honor	**f.** one from another country, or from space
7. _____ neighboring	**g.** a small circle or point
8. _____ overall	**h.** located near
9. _____ route	**i.** ride or run as fast as you can over a short distance
10. _____ sprint	**j.** a special award for doing something good

There is a saying in France that states: "The government could fall, the Louvre[1] could be broken into, or **aliens** could land on Earth, but if any of these things happened during the Tour de France, no one would notice." The Tour de France is the most famous **cycling** race in the world. The race, which is held in July every year, **consists of** twenty one-day stages, plus several rest days. The course follows a **clockwise route** around France, and often **neighboring** countries, including Luxembourg, Belgium, and Italy. The winner is the rider who completes all twenty stages of the race in the shortest **overall** time.

The Tour de France first started on July 1, 1903, when sixty cyclists left from in front of The Alarm Clock Café, just outside of Paris, and rode 467 kilometers to Lyon. The first race consisted of six legs, each of which was about 400 kilometers long. At that time there were no rest days—the winner was the rider who finished the race in the shortest total time. The winner of the first Tour de France, Maurice Garin, the most popular cyclist in France at that time, received 2,000 francs (about $350). It took him 94 hours and 33 minutes to ride all 2,428 kilometers of the race, three hours faster than the runner-up. Over the weeks during which the race was run, the idea of the Tour de France slowly caught on with the people of France. The race has been held every year since that time, except during the years of World Wars I and II.[2]

The Tour de France has developed several special honors for which racers compete. The highest **honor** is the "yellow jersey." Henri Desgranges,[3] the founder of the race, introduced the yellow jersey in 1919 to show the leading racer each day of the Tour de France. Each day, the officials who keep track of all of the riders' times compare each rider's total time up to that point. The racer with the lowest overall time wears the yellow jersey during the following day's race. Other honors include the "green jersey," which is given to the best **sprinter**, and the "polka dot jersey," a white jersey with red **dots**, for the best rider in the mountains along the route.

Over the years of the race, the competitors have gained a reputation for good sportsmanship. For example, if a lead rider falls off his bike, it is common for the following riders to slow down to allow the fallen rider to catch up. Some watchers are surprised by this, but as German rider Jan Ullrich, who came in runner-up in 2002 after waiting for winner Lance Armstrong, says, "Of course I would wait. If I would have won this race by taking advantage of someone's bad luck, then the race was not worth winning."

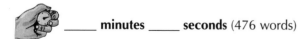

_____ **minutes** _____ **seconds** (476 words)

---

[1] **the Louvre** a famous museum in Paris
[2] **World Wars I and II** 1914–1918 and 1939–1945
[3] **Henri Desgranges (1865–1940)** French cyclist and journalist with French sports magazine *L'Auto*

Reading Comprehension

Circle the letter of the best answer.

1. What is this passage mainly about?

   a. famous Tour de France winners

   b. sportsmanship in the Tour de France

   c. the rules and history of the Tour de France

   d. techniques of the Tour de France cyclists

2. Who wins the Tour de France?

   a. the cyclist with the most points

   b. the cyclist with the shortest overall time

   c. the first cyclist to finish the race

   d. the cyclist with the polka dot jersey

3. Who was Henri Desgranges?

   a. a famous cyclist

   b. a café owner

   c. the man who won the first Tour de France

   d. the man who had the idea for the Tour de France

4. Today, the Tour de France is different from the original race because cyclists . . .

   a. ride in a clockwise direction.

   b. receive money as a prize.

   c. have days to rest during the race.

   d. have to ride for over 2,000 kilometers.

5. Who wears the yellow jersey?

   a. the fastest cyclist of the previous day

   b. the fastest overall cyclist up to that time

   c. the fastest cyclist over short distances

   d. the winner from the year before

Idioms

Find each idiom in the story.

1. **keep track of**—*keep accurate information about something*
   - The university uses special software to **keep track of** its students' grades.
   - For her diet, Melanie **keeps track of** how many calories she eats every day.

2. **take advantage of**—*to use an opportunity; to cheat someone*
   - I had a chance to buy a car for a low price, so I **took advantage of** it.
   - Ian doesn't know much about business, so people are always **taking advantage of** him.

3. **catch up (with/to someone)**—*reach someone in front of you by moving faster; reach someone else's level*
   - I had to walk slowly to let him **catch up with** me.
   - Philip missed a lot of school while he was sick, and had to study extra hard to **catch up to** the rest of the class.

Vocabulary Reinforcement

A. Circle the letter of the word or phrase that best matches the word(s) in *italics.*

1. According to a survey, more than fifty percent of Americans believe in *aliens.*

   a. dead people come   **b.** reading other   **c.** invisible people   **d.** people from space
   back to earth   people's minds

2. I'm not really very good at *sprinting.*

   a. cycling   **b.** running fast   **c.** swimming   **d.** sportsmanship

3. Which *way* did you take to get here?

   a. automatic   **b.** factor   **c.** circumstances   **d.** route

4. Meeting the president was *a special thing* for me.

   a. notorious   **b.** an incident   **c.** humble   **d.** an honor

5. I'm going to *take advantage of* the quiet time at work and go on vacation.

   a. stand a chance with   **b.** rely on   **c.** keep track of   **d.** use the opportunity of

6. He was walking so quickly that I had to ask him to slow down so I could *reach* him.

   a. make up with   **b.** catch up to   **c.** keep track of   **d.** take advantage of

7. Her dress is covered in black *dots.*

   a. circles   **b.** squares   **c.** stripes   **d.** dirt

8. Many rock bands *contain* three guitarists and a drummer.

   a. restore   **b.** honor   **c.** consist of   **d.** expect

B. Complete the passage with items from the box. One item is extra.

catch up	consists of	keep track of	neighboring	overall	clockwise	cycling

The Tour de France is the most famous (1)_____ race in the world. The race
follows a (2)_____ route around France, and some parts of the race may go into
(3)_____ countries like Belgium and Italy. The race (4)_____ twenty one-
day stages, but there are a few rest days for cyclists during these twenty days. The judges of
the race (5)_____ the time each rider takes to complete each stage of the race. At
the end of the race, the cyclist with the shortest (6)_____ time is the winner.

What Do You Think?

1. Do you agree with Jan Ullrich? Is sportsmanship more important than winning?

2. Is there any athlete in your country who is famous for his or her sportsmanship?

Review

A. Circle the correct answer for each question.

1. During the war, which is a government more likely to spend money on?　　**a.** the military　　**b.** the environment

2. Which of these is most likely to be arrested?　　**a.** an archaeologist　　**b.** a strangler

3. Which would most businessmen prefer to be?　　**a.** notorious　　**b.** honored

4. Who is more likely to take the Internet for granted?　　**a.** old people　　**b.** young people

5. Which country was America's ally during World War II?　　**a.** England　　**b.** Germany

6. An average person can last a _____ of six weeks without food.　　**a.** maximum　　**b.** minimum

7. Which number is more specific?　　**a.** 1,000　　**b.** 1,243

8. Which are you more likely to want to make up for?　　**a.** winning an award　　**b.** making a mistake

9. What are you more likely to do to catch up with someone?　　**a.** crawl　　**b.** sprint

10. Which of these jobs is more humble?　　**a.** president　　**b.** cleaner

B. Complete the paragraph with items from the box. Two items are extra.

| expected | funded | incident | made the headlines | media | neighboring |
| potentially | riddle | shocked | significant | visible | worship |

Archaeologists in England thought they had made an amazing discovery in July 2003, when tourists on a beach found ancient carvings on a large block of stone. The archaeologists believed that the discovery of the stone, which had been imported from Norway in the 1980s and used to make a wall, was (1)_____ very (2)_____. The carvings of two snakes, a dragon, and other shapes (3)_____ in the local (4)_____. Experts translated the stone to say, "This stone is for people who celebrate with fire."

However, two months later, the archaeologists were (5)_____ when the (6)_____ of the carvings was solved by a fifty-year-old local builder, Barry Luxton. The man, who had seen a photograph in a newspaper, told them that he was actually the one who had made the shapes—in 1995! Luxton said that over a period of three days in 1995 he had made the carvings for a celebration on a (7)_____ beach that was going to be held by a group of druids—people who (8)_____ nature. However, the block didn't end up being moved to the other beach and was eventually covered by sand. Recent bad weather blew the sand away, making the carvings (9)_____ again. Luxton was surprised; he really never (10)_____ that his work would become so famous.

C. Circle the odd one out in each group.

1. **a.** monument   **b.** sculpture   **c.** portrait   **d.** statue
2. **a.** crawl   **b.** route   **c.** sprint   **d.** cycle
3. **a.** incident   **b.** happening   **c.** series   **d.** event
4. **a.** keep track of   **b.** keep an eye on   **c.** make up for   **d.** watch out for
5. **a.** benefit   **b.** strangle   **c.** celebrate   **d.** honor
6. **a.** make sense of   **b.** work out   **c.** misunderstand   **d.** solve
7. **a.** humble   **b.** significant   **c.** important   **d.** major
8. **a.** a little   **b.** overall   **c.** complete   **d.** total
9. **a.** expect   **b.** hope   **c.** remember   **d.** predict
10. **a.** promise   **b.** lie   **c.** keep one's word   **d.** trust

D. Use the clues below to complete the crossword.

Across

1. I often _____ on my friends to help me.
5. a place where films are made
6. In total, there will be seven books in the *Harry Potter* _____.
7. The movie's _____ was almost $200 million.
9. _____, police still do not know who stole the statue in 1908. (3 words)
12. Koalas are _____ to Australia.
14. Pigeons like to sit on the _____ in the park.
15. a stick used by old people to help them walk
17. The town built this _____ to remember all the people killed in the last war.
18. for example, *E.T.*
19. _____ visits to the dentist are very important.

11. The tax cuts will only _____ the wealthy.
13. a small circle or spot
16. In the United States, the government's control over newspapers and other ___ is limited.

Down

1. They _____ the old house, and it looked like new.
2. Sam's parents _____ her college expenses.
3. Follow me. I know a shorter _____ to get there faster.
4. Although I haven't been there, I hear that restaurant has a great _____.
8. Our team doesn't _____ of winning the match on Sunday. (3 words)
10. The fireworks last night were _____.

Left-Handedness

Before You Read

Answer the following questions.

1. Are you left-handed? How many left-handed people do you know? _____

2. Do you know any famous people who are left-handed? _____

3. What percentage of people do you think are left-handed? _____

Target Vocabulary

Match each word with the best meaning.

1. _____ abnormal   **a.** to make a plan for something

2. _____ architect   **b.** feelings or ideas about someone or something

3. _____ attitude   **c.** (verb) change something for the worse; (noun) injury; harm

4. _____ damage   **d.** related to the body (rather than the mind)

5. _____ mental   **e.** related to the mind

6. _____ mild   **f.** job

7. _____ occupation   **g.** not serious; gentle

8. _____ physical   **h.** a trained professional who draws plans for buildings

9. _____ (to) design   **i.** someone who never eats animals

10. _____ vegetarian   **j.** unusual; not normal

27

Reading Passage Track 6

What do Leonardo da Vinci, Paul McCartney, and Albert Einstein have in common? They were all left-handed, along with other famous people including Pablo Picasso, Prince William, and Marilyn Monroe. In fact, an estimated 11 percent of Americans and Europeans are left-handed.

5 Most people around the world are right-handed. This fact also seems to have held true throughout history. In 1977, scientists studied works of art made at various times in history starting with cave drawings from 15,000 B.C. and ending with paintings from the 1950s. Most of the people shown in these works of art are right-handed, so scientists guessed that right-handedness has always been
10 common.

Many researchers claim to have found relationships between left-handedness and various **physical** and **mental** characteristics, such as blond hair, blue eyes, **vegetarianism**, and sleep difficulties. Other studies have found a higher-than-normal level of left-handed people in certain **occupations**, including professional
15 baseball and tennis players, **architects**, lawyers, as well as prisoners. However, some of these connections are very weak, and others haven't been proven.

What makes a person become right-handed rather than left-handed? As yet, no one really knows for sure. One simple idea suggests that people normally get right-handedness from their parents. Studies have found that two right-handed
20 parents have only a 9.5 percent chance of having a left-handed child, whereas two left-handed parents have a 26 percent chance of having a left-handed child. Another common theory is that left-handed people suffer **mild** brain **damage** during birth, which makes them left-handed. However, if this theory were true, it wouldn't explain why the percentage of left-handed people is so similar in every
25 society, when birth conditions vary so much from society to society.

Whatever the reasons behind it, people's **attitudes** toward left-handedness have changed a lot over the years. Statistics show that although 13 percent of young people (10–20 years old) are left-handed, only 6 percent of the elderly are left-handed. Left-handed children used to be punished until they began using their
30 right hand like other children, but today people who are left-handed are no longer looked down on nor are they considered **abnormal**. For most people today either case is perfectly acceptable. There are even a number of shops now that specialize in selling products **designed** for left-handed people, such as left-handed scissors, can openers, guitars, and even a left-handed camera.

35 In 1976, Left-Handers International, a group of left-handed people in Topeka, Kansas, in the United States, decided to start an annual event in order to clear up misunderstandings about left-handedness. They decided that August 13th is International Left-Handers Day, and to this day groups of left-handed people around the world celebrate their own special day.

 _____ **minutes** _____ **seconds** (444 words)

Reading Comprehension

Circle the letter of the best answer.

1. From studying works of art, scientists have learned that . . .

   a. left-handed people are better artists.

   b. most artists are left-handed.

   c. most people in history were right-handed.

   d. cave drawings were drawn using both hands.

2. What does the third paragraph describe?

   a. why people with certain characteristics are better at certain jobs

   b. reasons why left-handed people are better at some jobs

   c. links between left-handedness and certain occupations and characteristics

   d. why people are left-handed

3. What makes a person right-handed?

   a. the person's parents

   b. society

   c. the person's birth

   d. The reason is uncertain.

4. What can be assumed about the children of two left-handed parents?

   a. Most of them are left-handed.

   b. Most of them are right-handed.

   c. Most of them use both hands equally.

   d. Very few of them are right-handed.

5. Today, only 6 percent of the elderly are left-handed because left-handed people . . .

   a. can be treated by doctors today.

   b. die younger.

   c. are thought of as abnormal.

   d. were often forced to become right-handed.

Idioms

Find each idiom in the story.

1. **look down on/up to**—*think that someone is less/more important*
   - You shouldn't **look down on** others. All people should be treated equally.
   - Tom admired his older brother, and really **looked up to** him.

2. **as well as**—*and (used to mention another thing connected to the thing you are talking about)*
   - Please write your phone number here, **as well as** your name and address.
   - Many foreign web sites, **as well as** newspapers, are banned in that country.

3. **along with**—*together with; in addition to*
   - If you're not happy with your new clothes, you can return them, **along with** your receipt, and get your money back
   - When the company closed, the managers lost their jobs **along with** the regular workers.

Vocabulary Reinforcement

A. Circle the letter of the word or phrase that best completes the sentence.

1. He has his own company that _____ web sites.
   a. designs   **b.** damages   **c.** honors   **d.** neighbors

2. After her accident, she was left with terrible _____ injuries, and never walked again.
   a. occupation   **b.** vegetarian   **c.** physical   **d.** mental

3. The plans for his house were drawn by a famous _____.
   a. vegetarian   **b.** architect   **c.** archaeologist   **d.** lawyer

4. Experts predict that people born today will change _____ many times during their life.
   a. reputations   **b.** conditions   **c.** parents   **d.** occupations

5. _____ tigers, lions are one of the most popular animals in the zoo.
   a. Despite   **b.** On the other hand   **c.** Along with   **d.** Whereas

6. Don't forget, Mick is _____ so don't serve meat for dinner tonight.
   a. an architect   **b.** a vegetarian   **c.** a lawyer   **d.** a prisoner

7. Although my body feels fine, _____ I am very tired.
   a. artificially   **b.** mentally   **c.** abnormally   **d.** physically

8. The teacher had to speak to the student about his bad _____.
   a. shock   **b.** route   **c.** ally   **d.** attitude

B. Complete the passage with items from the box. One item is extra.

abnormal	so far	attitudes	looked down on	mild	occupations	damage

Although there have been some famous people who were left-handed, lefties (people who use their left hands more) used to be considered (1)_____. In fact, not only were lefties (2)_____ in the past, they were also trained to stop using their left hands and use their right instead. Today, (3)_____ have changed, and most people think that left-handedness is not wrong; it is just different. Some say left-handedness is genetic while others say it is caused by (4)_____ brain (5)_____, but (6)_____ nobody has found the real answer to this question.

What Do You Think?

1. What do you think causes left-handedness?
2. What do you think are some advantages and disadvantages of being left-handed?

Jennifer Lopez

Before You Read

Answer the following questions.

1. What is Jennifer Lopez famous for?

   _____

   _____

2. How is Lopez different from other entertainers?

   _____

   _____

3. Have you seen her movies or heard her music? If yes, which movies or songs?

   _____

   _____

Target Vocabulary

Match each word with the best meaning.

1. _____ entertainer
2. _____ line
3. _____ open (something)
4. _____ overcome
5. _____ passion
6. _____ perform
7. _____ perfume
8. _____ release
9. _____ tough
10. _____ will

a. succeed despite a difficult situation or problem
b. act or sing in front of an audience
c. a pleasant-smelling liquid, usually made from flowers
d. hard; difficult
e. strong emotion of happiness and excitement
f. a person who acts or sings
g. start (especially for movies)
h. determination to do something
i. a group of things for sale under the same brand name
j. sell publicly, like a movie, album, or book

Coming from the Bronx,[1] Jennifer Lopez knew from an early age it would be **tough** to achieve her dream. In an interview in 2002 she remembered, "I had such a **will** in me. I had such a **passion** in me. I could **overcome** my situation. But a lot of people will get beaten down and be held back by that." Lopez was not beaten
5   down by her situation. She worked hard dancing, singing, and acting in theaters and her hard work paid off with small roles in television and films.

Lopez's big breakthrough came in 1996 when she played the main role in the movie *Selena*. For this movie, Lopez got paid $1 million and became the highest paid Latin[2] actress of all time. Since then, she has had starring roles in several
10   successful movies, including *Out of Sight* (1998) with George Clooney.

Then, Lopez turned her attention toward music. In 1999, she **released** her first album, *On the 6*. Two songs from the album, "If You Had My Love" and "Waiting for Tonight," both reached number one on the Billboard music charts.[3] The album sold more than three million copies around the world.

15   After starring in *The Cell* (2000), Lopez released her second album, *J. Lo*, in 2001. The album went straight to the top of the Billboard chart. At the same time that her album came out, Lopez's new movie, *The Wedding Planner*, **opened** in theaters. It became the number one movie at the box office. This meant that Lopez was the first **entertainer** to ever have a number one album and a number
20   one movie at the same time! Like her first album, *J. Lo* went triple-platinum.

But her entertainment career was not the only thing Lopez focused on that year. 2001 was also the year Lopez started her own **line** of clothing, called *J. Lo*, and she married Cris Judd, a dancer who **performed** in her videos. The marriage did not last long, and Lopez and Judd divorced nine months later.

25   In 2002, Lopez starred in the films *Enough* and *Maid in Manhattan*. *Maid in Manhattan* became Lopez's biggest movie yet, earning $19 million during its first weekend in theaters. Lopez also put out her third album, *This Is Me . . . Then*, and the single "Jenny from the Block" hit number one for a week. To go with her line of clothing, Lopez introduced her own **perfume**.

30   In an interview, Lopez was asked if she planned to do more acting, singing, designing, or something new. She answered, "Yes, yes, yes, and yes! All of those things. I love making music, I love doing movies and all the other things. I think that everyone should do everything that they have a passion for."

 _____ **minutes** _____ **seconds** (457 words)

---

[1] **Bronx** a working-class area of New York City
[2] **Latin** from a Spanish (or Portuguese) speaking country
[3] **Billboard music charts** music sales ranking, published in *Billboard Magazine*

Reading Comprehension

Circle the letter of the best answer.

1. What is the main idea of the passage?

   a. Lopez is better at singing than acting.

   b. Lopez has done many things in her career.

   c. Lopez grew up in a poor family.

   d. Lopez has had many problems in her personal life.

2. Which of the following was most important in helping her career take off?

   a. acting in the movie *Selena*

   b. getting married to a dancer

   c. releasing a second album

   d. starring with George Clooney

3. Which is NOT true about Lopez?

   a. She has had several number one songs.

   b. She was a famous singer before she started acting.

   c. She wants to do other things besides acting and singing.

   d. She wanted to be an entertainer when she was young.

4. How is Lopez different from other actors who have made albums?

   a. Her albums are not popular outside the United States.

   b. She writes all of her own songs.

   c. She sings the main song in all of her movies.

   d. She has had a number one movie and album at the same time.

5. "... *J. Lo* went triple-platinum." What does this mean about the album?

   a. It was made by an actor or actress.

   b. It sold more than three million copies.

   c. It had songs from a movie on it.

   d. It sold most of its copies outside the United States.

Idioms

Find each idiom in the story.

1. **go with**—*suit or match well*
   - Do you think this yellow shirt **goes with** my purple pants?
   - The wine we had with dinner **went** well **with** the fish.

2. **pay off**—*have a valuable result*
   - It looks like all that exercise has been **paying off**. You look great!
   - In the end, all of his planning didn't **pay off** because his boss rejected his idea.

3. **hold back**—*keep from moving forward*
   - He could not **hold back** his dog as it tried to jump on the mail carrier.
   - She was **held back** a year in school because she couldn't read well.

■ Vocabulary Reinforcement

A. Circle the letter of the word or phrase that best completes the sentence.

1. I received an expensive bottle of _____ as a gift.
   a. line   **b.** passion   **c.** perfume   **d.** surroundings

2. He put his finger under his nose to _____ his sneeze.
   a. hold back   **b.** go with   **c.** take advantage of   **d.** keep track of

3. Many believe he is the most talented _____ of the century.
   a. environment   **b.** entertainer   **c.** vegetarian   **d.** alien

4. The second movie in the series will _____ next week.
   a. open   **b.** perform   **c.** release   **d.** sprint

5. The exam was so _____, some students couldn't complete it.
   a. passionate   **b.** spectacular   **c.** tough   **d.** notorious

6. I love your new tie. It really _____ that shirt.
   a. overcomes   **b.** performs   **c.** goes with   **d.** holds back

7. It takes a strong _____ to stop smoking.
   a. will   **b.** passion   **c.** mental   **d.** humble

8. Our business faced many problems, but we _____ them all.
   a. released   **b.** designed   **c.** damaged   **d.** overcame

B. Complete the passage with items from the box. One item is extra.

went with	line	paid off	passion	performed	released	tough

Jennifer Lopez knew very early that she would have a (1)_____ time becoming an actress. But she had a strong (2)_____ for singing and dancing, so she didn't give up. Finally, all of her work (3)_____ when she got a job in television. Several years later, she became the highest paid Latin actress in history when she (4)_____ in the movie *Selena*. After that, she (5)_____ several successful albums and started her own (6)_____ of clothing.

■ What Do You Think?

1. Which of the movies or songs from the passage do you know? What do you think of them?

2. Do you know any other entertainer with a career outside of acting and singing? What is this entertainer's other career?

Body Language

Before You Read

Answer the following questions.

1. Look at the pictures above.
   What can you tell about these people's feelings? _____

2. What do you think it means if someone crosses
   their arms when you are talking to them? _____

3. What kind of body language do you use
   when you are talking to people? _____

Target Vocabulary

Match each word with the best meaning.

1. _____ automatic
2. _____ circumstances
3. _____ factor
4. _____ gesture
5. _____ imply
6. _____ interpret
7. _____ offensive
8. _____ tone
9. _____ unconscious
10. _____ universal

a. a fact that one needs to consider
b. working by itself
c. conditions that make something happen
d. a body movement to show something
e. to suggest only indirectly
f. rude or impolite
g. the loudness or character of a voice
h. not thinking or sensing
i. found or done everywhere
j. to change the meaning of something in one language
   into another language

35

People use more than just words to communicate. In fact, some researchers claim that less than half of a spoken message's real meaning is in the words used in the message. They say that most of a message's meaning comes from understanding how the speaker uses things like **tone** of voice and body language.

5 Body language includes such things as the expression on the speaker's face, **gestures** the speaker makes with his or her hands, and the position of the speaker's body. Just as there are many different languages spoken around the world, there are many different ways for people to use body language, too. For example, gestures may **imply** different meanings in different cultures. Making a

10 "thumbs up" sign in America means "Great!" However, in Arab cultures, this gesture is extremely **offensive**. And in India, if listeners want to show speakers that they understand, the listeners will move their heads from side to side. In many Western countries, a similar gesture means "no."

Although many gestures can be **interpreted** differently by different cultures, there

15 are also many gestures that are almost **universally** interpreted the same way. For example, by and large a smile is understood as a sign of friendship or good will around the world. Also, using an open hand to gesture toward something is viewed as polite or friendly in most cultures.

There are also some forms of body language that can be universally read with the

20 meaning, "I am interested in you" or "I like you." Sometimes this kind of body language is used **unconsciously** between two people. These signs of interest include standing or sitting with both feet flat on the ground, mirroring or using the same gestures as the other person, and turning one's body to fully face the other person. In addition, a person's pupils[1] will **automatically** become wider

25 when they are interested in another person.

Body language that can be read with the meaning, "I am not interested in you" or "I don't like you," may include the following gestures: looking down or looking in another direction, leaning away from a person, crossing one's arms or legs, or tapping a foot or finger.

30 Body language experts point out one important thing. The person's culture is only one **factor** that can influence his or her use of body language. The time and place where the body language is being used can have a lot to do with a person's body language. If the person has had a bad day or if a meeting takes place in a crowded place, the body language a person uses may be very different than under

35 other **circumstances**.

_____ **minutes** _____ **seconds** (440 words)

---

[1] **pupil** the black circle in the center of the eye

Reading Comprehension

Circle the letter of the best answer.

1. What is the main idea of the passage?

   a. Body language is an important part of communication.

   b. Body language is less important for communication than spoken words.

   c. Body language can be extremely offensive.

   d. The best way to tell if someone likes you is by watching their body language.

2. What does the second paragraph describe?

   a. an example of a gesture not used in India

   b. differences in the meanings of gestures in different cultures

   c. how gestures completely change the meaning of a person's words

   d. useful gestures in Arab cultures

3. If the person you are talking to starts unconsciously copying your body language, what does this suggest about that person?

   a. She is interested in you.   **c.** She doesn't agree with you.

   b. She isn't interested in you.   **d.** She agrees with you.

4. Which gesture shows that you are not interested in the speaker?

   a. an increase in the size of your pupils   **c.** eating or drinking while the person speaks

   b. turning to face the speaker   **d.** not making eye contact with the speaker

5. Which of the following is NOT an example of body language?

   a. eye direction   **c.** head shaking

   b. voice tone   **d.** feet direction

Idioms

Find each idiom in the story.

1. **point out**—*make people look at something, or show them where it is*
   - She **pointed out** an error in the report.
   - He **pointed out** that the company cannot continue to lose money.

2. **have (something/nothing) to do with**—*be related in some way*
   - Kim's reaction to the news may **have something to do with** her mother being sick.
   - The color of someone's hair **has nothing to do with** how intelligent they are.

3. **by and large**—*in general; in most ways*
   - **By and large**, the students in the class did well on the exam.
   - Television, **by and large**, is how people get news from around the world.

Vocabulary Reinforcement

A. Circle the letter of the word or phrase that best matches the word(s) in *italics*.

1. He wasn't going to pay until I *told him* that I paid last time.

   a. had to do with him   **b.** kept track   **c.** took for granted   **d.** pointed out

2. The feeling of love is a *very widespread* human characteristic.

   a. universal   **b.** regular   **c.** mild   **d.** passionate

3. Many *things* contributed to the accident.

   a. aliens   **b.** factors   **c.** dots   **d.** gestures

4. That movie was really *offensive*.

   a. rude   **b.** romantic   **c.** funny   **d.** exciting

5. It really *has nothing to do with you*.

   a. wouldn't be   **b.** would be   **c.** isn't related to   **d.** would be
   interesting for you   difficult for you   you at all   damaging for you

6. *Generally*, dogs make great pets.

   a. As well as   **b.** To this day   **c.** As the name suggests   **d.** By and large

7. Although he didn't say it directly, the tone of his voice *suggested* that he was angry.

   a. implied   **b.** gestured   **c.** pointed out   **d.** announced

8. If you put a coin in that machine it washes your clothes *by itself*.

   a. well   **b.** quickly   **c.** automatically   **d.** carefully

B. Complete the passage with items from the box. One item is extra.

automatically	gestures	have to do with	interpreted	imply	unconscious	tone

When people meet and talk, they are using not only words, but also the (1)_____
of their voice and their body language to communicate. Sometimes people use body
language consciously to add meaning to their words, but other body language may be
(2)_____. For example, a person may (3)_____ start tapping his or her
foot while talking with someone. This body language could be (4)_____ as
meaning "I am not interested in talking with you." Other (5)_____ that
(6)_____ not being interested in others include crossed arms, leaning away from
others, and not looking at the speaker.

What Do You Think?

1. What advice about body language in your country would you give to a foreign tourist?

2. How can the tone of someone's voice show what they are thinking?

Cosmetic Surgery

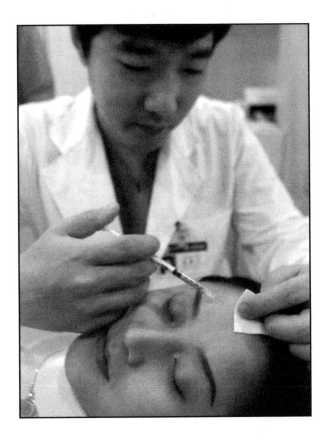

Before You Read

Answer the following questions.

1. What makes a man handsome in your country? What makes a woman beautiful?

   _____

   _____

2. What can a person do to make themselves more beautiful?

   _____

   _____

3. Is cosmetic surgery popular in your country? What kinds of cosmetic surgery are popular?

   _____

   _____

   _____

Target Vocabulary

Match each word with the best meaning.

1. _____ complain
2. _____ inject
3. _____ institute
4. _____ involve; be involved in
5. _____ patient
6. _____ procedure
7. _____ rapid
8. _____ repair
9. _____ scar
10. _____ temporary

a. consist of; including; take part in

b. put something into the body with a needle

c. a correct way of doing something, often in medicine

d. to speak about pain, or something that is wrong

e. fix something that has been damaged

f. a person who receives medical treatment from a doctor

g. quick or sudden (usually of a change)

h. a mark on the skin that remains after an injury has healed

i. an organization, especially one for education or research

j. lasting for a short period (opposite: permanent—lasting or meant to last forever, or for a long time)

Reading Passage Track 9

Doctors at the **Institute** of Reconstructive Surgery in Guadalajara, Mexico, were shocked at what they found when Maria Concepcion Lopez, a mother of four, came to them **complaining** of pain following a cosmetic surgery operation she had had. Maria was just the first of many **patients** they saw who showed strange
5 symptoms following cosmetic surgery.

What all of these unlucky women, as well as 430 others in the Mexican city of Guadalajara, had in common was that they had all had medical treatment from a woman called Myriam Yukie Gaona, paying her up to $1,000 a day for the treatment. "She said she'd make us look like Barbie dolls,"[1] said Ms. Lopez.
10 However, Ms. Gaona was a medically untrained ex-dancer who passed herself off as a doctor and treated hundreds of women before she was finally arrested. She claimed to be able to perform cosmetic surgery, but instead **injected** dangerous chemicals into her victims, leaving many permanently **scarred**. The Mexican media called her "La Matabellas," the beauty killer, although her lawyer said ". . . but
15 she didn't kill anyone—and none of them are beautiful anyway."

Fortunately, not all plastic surgery is as unsuccessful as that of the victims in Guadalajara, and most doctors who perform plastic surgery are far more skilled than Ms. Gaona. There are two kinds of plastic surgery—reconstructive surgery, which is done to **repair** damage caused by illness or accident; and cosmetic
20 surgery, which is done to change features of the body that a person doesn't like. Cosmetic surgery is becoming increasingly popular in the United States—according to the American Society of Plastic Surgeons (the industry association for cosmetic surgeons), nearly 6.6 million cosmetic surgery **procedures** were carried out in 2002.

25 The most commonly performed procedures are breast augmentation (breast enlargement), lipoplasty (fat removal), and face lifts (to remove wrinkles[2] on the face), all of which **involve** surgery. However, one non-surgical technique is **rapidly** increasing in popularity. It involves an injection of botulism toxin (Botox®), a poison which **temporarily** paralyzes nerves. A ten-minute treatment of Botox,
30 injecting it into the wrinkles in the forehead, paralyzes the muscles there, and can cause wrinkles to disappear for up to four months. In the first year of this treatment, over half a million Americans tried it, and in 2002 there were over a million Botox procedures performed.

Many people think that cosmetic surgery is for women, and to an extent this is
35 true—85 percent of patients in 2002 were female. But, there were almost a million American men who had cosmetic surgery in 2002. Why is cosmetic surgery so popular? In the words of one man who has had several treatments: "People all think that I'm in my early thirties," he says. ". . . when we're talking, I like to tell them my actual age and watch their shocked reactions."

 _____ **minutes** _____ **seconds** (476 words)

---

[1] **Barbie® dolls** beautiful female dolls for young girls, made by Mattel, Inc.
[2] **wrinkles** lines which people get on their skin as they grow old

40   Unit 9

Reading Comprehension

Circle the letter of the best answer.

1. Which sentence about the women in Guadalajara is true?

   a. Their doctor was not a real doctor.

   b. They used to be dancers.

   c. They paid a thousand dollars for their operations.

   d. Their cosmetic surgeon worked at the Institute of Reconstructive Surgery.

2. Face lifts are . . .

   a. a type of reconstructive surgery.

   b. used to remove fat.

   c. non-surgical.

   d. probably performed most often on older people.

3. Which parts of the body does Botox affect?

   a. fat

   b. nerves

   c. muscles

   d. scars

4. What procedure would be best for someone who had been scarred in a fire?

   a. cosmetic surgery

   b. reconstructive surgery

   c. lipoplasty

   d. Botox

5. The majority of cosmetic surgery procedures performed in the United States are . . .

   a. changes to people's noses.

   b. performed in Guadalajara.

   c. performed on women.

   d. non-surgical.

Idioms

Find each idiom in the story.

1. look like—*look the same as someone or something; seem to be*
   • Alice **looks like** her mother.
   • The other apartment **looks like** a nicer place to live.

2. pass (oneself/something) off as—*try to make people believe you are something you are not, or something is something it is not*
   • Although he didn't know much about the subject, he often tried to **pass himself off as** an expert.
   • She was arrested after trying to **pass** fakes **off as** real paintings.

3. to an extent—*something is partly true, but not completely true*
   • I agree with you **to an extent**.
   • **To an extent**, most people supported the government's decision.

Vocabulary Reinforcement

A. Circle the letter of the word or phrase that best completes the sentence.

1. After the fire, he was left with permanent _____.
   a. repairs   **b.** harms   **c.** scars   **d.** illnesses

2. My car won't start. I need to take it to be _____.
   a. damaged   **b.** injected   **c.** released   **d.** repaired

3. She works for _____ that researches cancer.
   a. a procedure   **b.** an institute   **c.** a wrinkle   **d.** a treatment

4. James really _____ his brother. It's hard to tell them apart.
   a. goes with   **b.** looks up to   **c.** looks like   **d.** passes himself off as

5. This food tastes terrible. I'm going to _____.
   a. complain   **b.** claim   **c.** point out   **d.** offensive

6. I think you're right _____, but I don't completely agree with you.
   a. along with   **b.** to an extent   **c.** point of view   **d.** whereas

7. The last ten years has been a period of very _____ change in the computer industry.
   a. offensive   **b.** rapid   **c.** notorious   **d.** potential

8. After he broke his back, he was _____, and had to use a wheelchair.
   a. wrinkled   **b.** scarred   **c.** plastic   **d.** paralyzed

B. Complete the passage with items from the box. One item is extra.

injected   involving   look like   passed herself off as   procedure   temporarily   patients

There was a terrible case in Mexico (1)_____ many women who complained after receiving cosmetic surgery. In this case, patients received cosmetic treatment from an ex-dancer who (2)_____ a doctor. For the treatment, the woman (3)_____ dangerous chemicals into her (4)_____. Actually, this (5)_____ is similar to another safe kind of cosmetic treatment using injections of a chemical called Botox. Botox paralyzes muscles in the face and will (6)_____ remove wrinkles for up to four months.

What Do You Think?

1. Do you know of any famous people who have had cosmetic surgery?
2. What are the main reasons why people have cosmetic surgery?

Oil Spills

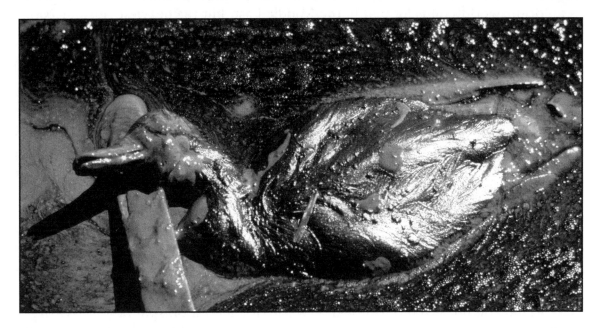

Before You Read

Answer the following questions.

1. Which oil companies are famous in your country?

2. Have there been any large oil spills reported in the news recently? If yes, where?

3. How do you think most oil spills are caused?

Target Vocabulary

Match each word with the best meaning.

1. _____ affect   **a.** necessary; required

2. _____ disaster   **b.** lasting for a long time (opposite: short-term)

3. _____ essential   **c.** something very bad that happens, usually causing a lot of damage

4. _____ float   **d.** not deep

5. _____ harm   **e.** to cause or allow liquid to fall from a container

6. _____ leak   **f.** (for a liquid or gas) escape through a hole or crack in a container

7. _____ long-term   **g.** cause an effect

8. _____ occur   **h.** rest or move at the top of, and supported by, liquid or air

9. _____ shallow   **i.** happen

10. _____ spill   **j.** damage

Oil is **essential** for modern life—apart from its use in transportation, it is also used in making fertilizers,[1] plastics, and many other products. About 64 percent of the world's oil is located in the Middle East, but the heaviest consumers of oil are Europe, America, and Japan. The problem lies in getting the oil from the

5 countries that produce it to the countries that consume it. This is mainly done using oil tankers. There are roughly 4,000 oil tankers in use today, and every day more than 100 million tons of oil is shipped. Usually this oil is shipped safely and with no problems, but occasionally there is a **disaster**.

Every year millions of tons of oil are **spilled** into the ocean. Although this is only

10 a small percentage of the total amount shipped around the world each year, this spilled oil can have terrible effects on ocean life, including the coastlines[2] where the oil washes up onto shore. Some of the largest spills in history have been caused by oil tankers running into each other or by an oil tanker running aground[3] in **shallow** water. After these spills, officials try to discover who or what

15 was at fault to help prevent similar accidents in the future.

One of the worst oil spills in history **occurred** along the Alaskan coastline in 1989, when the *Exxon Valdez* tanker ran aground off the coast of Alaska, spilling 42 million liters of oil. Although it wasn't the largest oil spill of all time, the Exxon Valdez disaster was terrible because it occurred in such a sensitive natural

20 area. In this spill, the tanker's captain, who was tired from overwork and drinking alcohol, had gone to take a rest. He gave control of the ship to another sailor, who was unfamiliar with the route the ship was taking. The ship ran onto Bligh Reef, a natural underwater rock wall near the Alaskan coast. Damaged by the reef, the ship **leaked** oil out into the ocean. More than 1,600 kilometers of

25 coastline were affected by the oil spill. Some scientists who studied nature in the area estimate that 580,000 birds and 5,500 otters died as a result of the oil from the spill covering their skin. Smaller shellfish and other sea creatures living on the ocean floor were also **affected**, and these creatures were later eaten by seals, whales, and other animals.

30 The most oil ever spilled was actually released on purpose as part of the Iraqi war plan during the Gulf War in 1991. Almost a million tons of oil were released into the Persian Gulf. This oil covered 1,500 square kilometers of water in the Persian Gulf, and also damaged 650 kilometers of the coastlines of Kuwait and Saudi Arabia. In some places, oil **floating** on the water was measured to be 43

35 centimeters thick. Water birds, water plants, and fish were all seriously **harmed** by the oil. The **long-term** effects of this act on the food chain in the area are likely to cause problems far into the future.

 _____ **minutes** _____ **seconds** (508 words)

---

[1] **fertilizers** chemicals or natural materials used to help plants grow
[2] **coastline** the land along an ocean or sea
[3] **run aground** become stuck on sand, rocks, etc.

Reading Comprehension

Circle the letter of the best answer.

1. Which country is NOT among the largest consumers of oil?

   a. Germany

   b. Iraq

   c. Japan

   d. the United States

2. According to the passage, oil spills . . .

   a. may involve one or two tankers.

   b. usually occur during war time.

   c. are usually harmless.

   d. are caused by wildlife.

3. Why did the sailor run the *Exxon Valdez* aground?

   a. He was tired.

   b. He was drunk.

   c. He did not know the area.

   d. He was watching the otters at the time.

4. What sentence about the Alaskan spill is true?

   a. More otters were killed than birds.

   b. Birds died from eating the oil.

   c. It was the worst oil spill of all time.

   d. Seals and whales were affected by eating smaller sea animals.

5. Which country was responsible for dumping oil into the Persian Gulf?

   a. Iraq

   b. Kuwait

   c. Saudi Arabia

   d. the United States

Idioms

Find each idiom in the story.

1. **at fault**—*responsible or to blame for a bad situation*
   - The drunk driver was **at fault** for the accident.
   - The two neighbors went to court to decide who was **at fault**.

2. **run into**—*crash into something; meet someone by chance*
   - The car **ran into** a tree because the driver fell asleep.
   - Francesca **ran into** some friends at the rodeo.

3. **on purpose**—*with reason; not by accident*
   - Sung-Taek left the door open **on purpose**. It was hot inside.
   - I didn't hit you **on purpose**. It was an accident.

Vocabulary Reinforcement

A. Circle the letter of the word or phrase that best completes the sentence.

1. No one was _____. It was an accident.
   a. at fault   **b.** on purpose   **c.** unconscious   **d.** offensive

2. While I was out shopping, I _____ an old friend.
   a. took advantage of   **b.** broke into   **c.** ran into   **d.** looked down on

3. Water is _____ for humans to live.
   a. abnormal   **b.** permanent   **c.** leaked   **d.** essential

4. The _____ effects of the government's decision won't be known for many years.
   a. short-term   **b.** long-term   **c.** temporary   **d.** period

5. I can't cycle to work this morning. There is a hole in my tire, and all the air has _____ out.
   a. leaked   **b.** spilled   **c.** fallen   **d.** floated

6. The river is quite _____ here, and you can walk across it.
   a. essential   **b.** spectacular   **c.** specific   **d.** shallow

7. If steel is heavier than water, why are ships able to _____ on the sea?
   a. leak   **b.** sink   **c.** float   **d.** spill

8. Although they had guns, the bank robbers didn't _____ anyone in the robbery.
   a. steal   **b.** harm   **c.** affect   **d.** inject

B. Complete the passage with items from the box. One item is extra.

affected	disaster	floated	on purpose	ran into	spilled	occurred

Millions of tons of oil are shipped over the oceans in tankers every year. Sometimes lots of this oil may be (1)_____ into the ocean. One terrible spill (2)_____ when the *Exxon Valdez* tanker (3)_____ a reef in shallow water, and millions of liters of oil leaked out of the ship. This accident created a (4)_____ in the area because plants and animals in the ocean and along the coast were (5)_____. However, the largest oil spill in history was spilled (6)_____ as part of Iraq's war plan during the 1991 Gulf War.

What Do You Think?

1. What can people do to reduce the amount of oil they use?
2. What can people do to help protect ocean life?

Review

A. Circle the correct answer for each question.

1. Which kind of problem would most people prefer?   **a.** temporary   **b.** permanent
2. Which kind of movie is more popular?   **a.** offensive   **b.** entertaining
3. Which of these is more essential for people?   **a.** water   **b.** university
4. Which of these does an architect design?   **a.** buildings   **b.** machines
5. Which of these floats?   **a.** a stone   **b.** a bottle
6. Which of these is more useful to a deaf person?   **a.** tone   **b.** gestures
7. Which would most people prefer to overcome?   **a.** problems   **b.** success
8. Where do most people get scars?   **a.** in a store   **b.** in accidents
9. Which are you more likely to see in a hospital?   **a.** patients   **b.** performers
10. Murder is killing someone _____.   **a.** by accident   **b.** on purpose

B. Complete the paragraph with items from the box. Two items are extra.

abnormal	affected	at fault	complained	damage	floating
long-term	occurred	patients	physical	releasing	shallow

One of the most terrible environmental disasters of the last fifty years was that which (1)_____ in Minamata Bay in Japan in the 1950s and 1960s. Minamata is a rural farming and fishing area on the Japanese island of Kyushu. It was also the home of a large chemical factory owned by the Chisso chemical company.

In 1956, a five-year-old girl in the area was taken to the hospital with brain (2)_____ as well as (3)_____ problems, such as being unable to walk, and (4)_____ speech. This girl was one of the first of thousands of (5)_____ to show similar symptoms. Doctors were at first unable to determine the cause of the problem, which became known as Minamata disease, but finally they worked it out. Over a long period of time, the Chisso factory had been (6)_____ alkyl mercury (a chemical) into the bay. This chemical then (7)_____ the fish of the bay, which were then eaten by the residents, causing poisoning.

The villagers (8)_____ to the company, but for a long time the company refused to believe that it was (9)_____. Finally, the villagers were able to receive money from the company and the government, but the (10)_____ effects of the poisoning continue to this day.

C. Circle the odd one out in each group.

1. **a.** long-term   **b.** permanent   **c.** temporary   **d.** forever

2. **a.** spill   **b.** occur   **c.** float   **d.** leak

3. **a.** architect   **b.** performer   **c.** entertainer   **d.** musician

4. **a.** by and large   **b.** along with   **c.** in addition to   **d.** as well as

5. **a.** attitude   **b.** damage   **c.** disaster   **d.** harm

6. **a.** have to do with   **b.** involve   **c.** affect   **d.** interpret

7. **a.** will   **b.** harm   **c.** attitude   **d.** passion

8. **a.** limited   **b.** general   **c.** common   **d.** universal

9. **a.** eventual   **b.** fast   **c.** rapid   **d.** quick

10. **a.** look like   **b.** seem   **c.** hold back   **d.** pass oneself off as

D. Use the clues below to complete the crossword.

Across

4. The weather has been very _____ this season—not too hot or too cold.

6. The typhoon caused $100 million worth of _____.

7. When making ice cream, fresh milk is _____.

9. You shouldn't _____ poor people. (3 words)

12. In theory, you can build a boat from anything that _____.

13. related to the body, not the mind

15. The changes are only _____—not permanent.

17. His words are friendly, but his _____ is rude.

18. If you're not careful, you'll _____ your coffee.

Down

1. suggest something rather than saying it clearly

2. The car accidentally _____ a wall. (2 words)

3. She has a real _____ for music.

5. Many movie stars start their own _____ of clothes.

8. It will take years to discover the _____ effects of the decision.

10. It's easier to succeed if your _____ is strong.

11. I need to _____ my bicycle. It's broken.

12. High salaries are only one _____ behind high prices.

14. relating to the mind

15. I got this _____ falling off my bike.

16. That new movie _____ next week.

Delivering the Mail 11

Before You Read

Answer the following questions.

1. How often do you send letters (not e-mails)? Who do you send them to?

_____

_____

2. Do you know anyone who collects stamps?

_____

_____

3. Which country do you think had the first postal service? How long ago do you think it started?

_____

_____

Target Vocabulary

Match each word with the best meaning.

1. _____ accessible   **a.** set up; found; start

2. _____ empire   **b.** easy to reach or get into

3. _____ establish   **c.** help or encourage something to happen

4. _____ holy   **d.** a group of nations ruled by a central government

5. _____ intend   **e.** coming from or connected with God or a particular religion

6. _____ jealous   **f.** one who receives something

7. _____ profit   **g.** plan (to do something)

8. _____ promote   **h.** damage something completely

9. _____ recipient   **i.** money made after the cost of expenses is taken away

10. _____ ruin   **j.** feeling angry because someone has something you don't, or wants something you have

The first organized system for sending messages began in Egypt around 1500 B.C. This system developed because the pharaohs frequently needed to send messages up and down the Nile River in order to keep their **empire** running smoothly. Later, the Persians[1] developed a more efficient system for sending messages using men
5 and horses. Message carriers rode along the road system stretching from one end of the Persian Empire to the other. Along these roads, fresh men and horses waited at special stations to take and pass along any messages that needed to be sent. The stations where riders passed messages back and forth were built 23 kilometers apart, so the men and horses were able to travel quickly between them. The
10 Romans later took this idea and improved it by using a more advanced and extensive road system.

In China, however, Kublai Khan[2] had built up his own system for delivering messages. This system worked in the same basic way as the Roman system. The difference was that Kublai Khan kept 300,000 horses along the roads of his
15 delivery lines. There were over 10,000 stations where a message would be passed from one rider to another with a fresh horse. In this way, Kublai Khan could receive messages from anywhere in the country in only a few days.

It wasn't until the 1500s that a well-organized postal system appeared again in Europe. One family, the von Taxis family, gained the right to deliver mail for the
20 **Holy** Roman Empire (most of Italy) and parts of Spain. This family continued to carry mail, both government and private, throughout Europe for almost 300 years.

In 1653, a French man, Renouard de Velayer, **established** a system for delivering post in Paris. Postal charges at that time were paid by the **recipient,** but de Velayer's system was unique by allowing the sender to pre-pay[3] the charges, in a
25 similar way to the modern stamp. Unfortunately, de Velayer's system came to an end when **jealous** competitors put live mice in his letter boxes, **ruining** his business. Eventually, government-controlled postal systems took over from private postal businesses, and by the 1700s government ownership of most postal systems in Europe was an accepted fact of life.

30 The thing that all these early systems had in common was that they were quite expensive for public use, and were **intended** for use by the government and the wealthy. However, in 1840, an English schoolteacher named Roland Hill suggested introducing postage stamps, and a postal rate based on weight. This resulted in lowering postal rates, encouraging more people to use the system. His idea helped
35 the British postal system begin to earn **profits** as early as 1850. Soon after that many other countries took up Mr. Hill's idea, and letter writing became **accessible** to anyone who could write. Today, the Roland Hill awards are given each year to "encourage and reward fresh ideas which help **promote** philately" (stamp collecting).

_____ **minutes** _____ **seconds** (490 words)

---

[1] **Persian** from Persia, now called Iran
[2] **Kublai Khan (1215–1294)** ruler of the Mongol Empire, covering Mongolia and China
[3] **pre-pay** the prefix "pre-" means "before." Pre-pay means pay before.

Reading Comprehension

Circle the letter of the best answer.

1. What is NOT discussed in the passage?

   a. earliest methods of sending messages   **c.** the origin of postal stamps

   b. the first European postal system   **d.** the future of mail delivery

2. Which of these postal systems did NOT rely on roadside stations and horses?

   a. Egyptian   **c.** Roman

   b. Persian   **d.** Chinese

3. Which sentence about Renouard de Velayer is true?

   a. His was a government-controlled system.   **c.** His competitors destroyed his business.

   b. His system lasted for hundreds of years.   **d.** In his system, the person who received the letter paid the postage fees.

4. Which of the systems mentioned in the passage was most like the postal system today?

   a. Egyptian   **c.** de Velayer's

   b. Chinese   **d.** von Taxis's

5. What was Roland Hill's greatest achievement?

   a. He made letter writing accessible to the average person.

   b. He made stamp collecting a popular hobby.

   c. He made a lot of money for the British postal system.

   d. He won an award for letter writing.

Idioms

Find each idiom in the story.

1. **take over**—*take control of*
   * Germany **took over** Poland in World War II.
   * Can you **take over** my job while I'm away on vacation?

2. **come to an end**—*finish; stop*
   * Eventually, all good things **come to an end**.
   * Many people were crying when the movie **came to an end**.

3. **in touch (with)**—*in contact with; keeping regular communication with*
   * He hasn't been **in touch with** his parents for several years.
   * We've **lost touch with** each other since we left school.

Vocabulary Reinforcement

A. Circle the letter of the word or phrase that best completes the sentence.

1. Let me know as soon as you've decided what you _____ to do.
   a. promote **b.** intend **c.** ruin **d.** establish

2. That town used to be a great place, but all the tourists have _____ it.
   a. ruined **b.** established **c.** repaired **d.** implied

3. Linda feels _____ when her boyfriend talks to other women.
   a. holy **b.** essential **c.** jealous **d.** passion

4. She was really happy to be the _____ of the award.
   a. profit **b.** prize **c.** entertainer **d.** recipient

5. This church has been a _____ place for hundreds of years.
   a. shallow **b.** holy **c.** jealous **d.** long-term

6. Despite what they may say, most companies are in business to make a _____.
   a. profit **b.** take over **c.** disaster **d.** budget

7. The smaller company was _____ by the larger corporation.
   a. profited **b.** come to an end **c.** taken over **d.** in touch

8. That conference is a good chance for businesses to _____ their products.
   a. merchandise **b.** promote **c.** profit **d.** affect

B. Complete the passage with items from the box. One item is extra.

accessible   established   keep in touch with   intended   recipient   empire   came to an end

Several ancient cultures (1)_____ good postal systems so that rulers could (2)_____ very distant parts of their kingdoms. For example, rulers in Egypt, Rome, and China all had systems for delivering messages. But when the Roman (3)_____ finally (4)_____, the Roman system for delivering messages disappeared in Europe. One thing all of these early mail systems had in common was that they were only (5)_____ for the rulers and very rich people. However, today mail systems are cheap enough to be (6)_____ to everyone.

What Do You Think?

1. Do you think your country has a good postal service? Why or why not?

2. Do you think that e-mail will eventually replace letters, or do you think that people will always write letters?

Speed Dating

Before You Read

Answer the following questions.

1. What are the most common ways to meet someone in your country?

2. What do people usually do on a first date?

3. Look at the title of this reading. What do you think it means? ·

Target Vocabulary

Match each word with the best meaning.

1. _____ community
2. _____ conventional
3. _____ episode
4. _____ exchange
5. _____ flow
6. _____ impression
7. _____ key
8. _____ participate
9. _____ pressure
10. _____ scan

a. stress; a feeling of being pushed to do something

b. a group of people who live in the same place

c. move smoothly, like water

d. important factor

e. one in a series of events

f. take part in an activity

g. usual; normal; in use for a long time

h. swap

i. look through something quickly to find important or interesting information

j. one's thoughts or feelings towards someone or something, after having met him, her, or it

Reading Passage Track 12

You are the first to arrive at the table in the back corner of the restaurant. As you sit down, a handsome stranger comes to the table and takes the seat across from you. You read his name on his nametag, "Jason." Once he is seated, a bell rings and your date begins!

5 As you **scan** your list of conversation topics, the man across the table asks about your hobbies. From there, the conversation naturally **flows** back and forth from your interests to his interests to your job to his job. You are both careful not to ask questions that are too personal, such as "Where do you live?" or "What's your last name?" Then the bell rings again. It's time to move on. As you make
10 your way to the next table, you quickly mark your date card. You write the man's name on the card. Under the question "Would you like to meet again for a real date?", you mark "yes." Then you take a seat for your next date.

Welcome to the world of speed dating! This is the latest way for single people to meet other people they might like to date without the **pressure** associated with the
15 **conventional** dating scene. Many businesses offering speed dating services have become especially popular in the United States, England, and Canada. These businesses organize events where **participants** can have dozens of quick dates all on the same night. Each speed date is less than ten minutes, and some services limit each date to only three minutes. This gives people just enough time to make
20 an **impression**, so that each person in the "date" can decide if they want to meet the other again. If both people mark "yes" on the date card, the service will arrange for the people to contact one another to arrange a real date.

The idea for speed dating came from Yaacov Deyo of Los Angeles. In 1999, he wanted to provide an alternative way for his students to get together other than
25 using blind dates arranged through family or friends. His speed dating idea was so successful, that it quickly spread to other **communities** across the United States. Deyo and his wife also wrote a book, *SpeedDating: A Timesaving Guide to Finding Your Lifelong Love*, to teach other people the **keys** to successful speed dating. Then businesses were set up to try to cash in on the popularity of speed
30 dating. And after a popular television sit-com[1] did an **episode** on speed dating, dating services across the United States really took off.

Like any date, speed dating does not always work out. But most services claim to have at least a 50 percent success rate for daters. And, in the case of Erik and Denise from Milwaukee,[2] their night of speed dating eventually led to marriage.
35 But the funny thing is they never actually had a speed date together. They just saw each other at a speed dating event and decided to **exchange** phone numbers at the end of the evening.

 _____ **minutes** _____ **seconds** (507 words)

---

[1] **sit-com** situation comedy (a type of funny TV series)
[2] **Milwaukee** a large city in Wisconsin, USA

Reading Comprehension

Circle the letter of the best answer.

1. How is speed dating different from conventional dating?

   a. The dates are very short.

   b. It usually isn't possible to meet the person again.

   c. The couples do many activities on one date.

   d. The people usually know each other quite well.

2. What would be a suitable question for speed dating?

   a. Where do you live?

   b. What's your last name?

   c. What sports do you like?

   d. What's your phone number?

3. How long might it take a person to complete ten speed dates?

   a. ten minutes

   b. one evening

   c. one week

   d. ten days

4. Who is Deyo?

   a. a man who has had many speed dates

   b. the inventor of speed dating

   c. a man who got married after speed dating

   d. the president of a speed dating company

5. Which event led to a rapid rise in speed dating in the United States?

   a. a national speed dating event

   b. a television broadcast

   c. the marriage of Erik and Denise

   d. the publication of a book in Milwaukee

Idioms

Find each idiom in the story.

1. **cash in on**—*earn money from some idea or trend; take advantage of something to make money from it*
   - Most entertainers try to **cash in on** their fame while they are popular.
   - The local people were able to **cash in on** the tourists who flooded the island every summer.

2. **move on**—*finish one thing and start something new; continue to the next thing*
   - All right, if everyone has finished reading the passage, let's **move on** to the questions.
   - After all the plants on the farm were eaten, the locusts **moved on** to the next field.

3. **one another**—*each other*
   - We haven't spoken to **one another** in years.
   - We depend on **one another** because we each have different skills.

Vocabulary Reinforcement

A. Circle the letter of the word or phrase that best completes the sentence.

1. A saying in English says, "You don't get a second chance to make a first _____."

    a. pressure   **b.** community   **c.** episode   **d.** impression

2. The police _____ the faces of the crowd, looking for the criminal.

    a. scanned   **b.** flowed   **c.** caught up with   **d.** looked like

3. New York and San Francisco both have very large Chinese _____.

    a. conventions   **b.** episodes   **c.** communities   **d.** procedures

4. The _____ to being a good piano player is lots of practice.

    a. key   **b.** factor   **c.** reason   **d.** effect

5. My wife's really into alternative films, but I'm into more _____ movies.

    a. offensive   **b.** holy   **c.** pressure   **d.** conventional

6. There was a great _____ of that series on TV last night.

    a. empire   **b.** episode   **c.** impression   **d.** tone

7. The river _____ down from the mountains into the sea.

    a. flows   **b.** spills   **c.** leaks   **d.** floats

8. Many people tried to _____ the idea of buying Internet names and then reselling them for more money.

    a. profit   **b.** cash in on   **c.** make a fortune   **d.** move on

B. Complete the passage with items from the box. One item is extra.

cash in on   exchange   impression   move on   participate   pressure   one another

Speed dating is a new way for single people to meet each other without the
(1)_____ of going on a lot of dates. At a speed-dating party, a person can
(2)_____ in many short dates on the same evening. Couples only talk to each
other long enough to get a(n) (3)_____ of (4)_____ before they
(5)_____ to the next date. The couples do not (6)_____ any personal
information during these dates, but if both want to see each other again, the speed-dating
company will put them in contact with each other.

What Do You Think?

1. What do you think about speed dating? How much can you find out about someone in three minutes?

2. Would you like to try speed dating? Why or why not?

Mystery Mansion

Before You Read

Answer the following questions.

1. Are there any interesting or unusual houses in your country?

   _____

2. What is the largest house you've ever been in? How many rooms do you think it had?

   _____

3. Do you know anything about the house pictured above? What do you think is the story behind it?

   _____

Target Vocabulary

Match each word with the best meaning.

1. _____ confuse
2. _____ decorate
3. _____ grief
4. _____ haunt
5. _____ heir
6. _____ insane
7. _____ rifle
8. _____ rights
9. _____ tragedy
10. _____ weapon

a. a tool used to harm or kill

b. make it difficult to know which way or answer is right

c. make something more beautiful by adding things to it

d. a type of long gun

e. great sadness

f. a sad event; disaster

g. mentally ill; acting very strangely

h. visit as a ghost

i. legal permission to do or make something and make money from

j. someone who inherits someone's money or property when that person dies

Many people decide to rebuild or **redecorate** their homes at some point, and sometimes the job takes longer than expected. Very rarely, however, does it take as long as one house in the United States. The Winchester house, owned by Sarah Winchester in San Jose, California, was rebuilt twenty-four hours a day for over
5 thirty-eight years!

The remarkable story of the Winchester house began in 1862 when Sarah Pardee of Boston married William Winchester, the **heir** to the Winchester fortune. William was the son of Oliver Winchester who owned the **rights** to the Winchester **Rifle**, one of the most popular **weapons** of the time.

10 In 1866, Sarah and William had a daughter, Annie, who died from a disease as a baby. Sarah was overcome with **grief** at the death of her child, and took many years to recover. Then, **tragedy** struck Sarah again when William died of a disease in 1881. Although she inherited $20 million in savings, and an income of a thousand dollars a day, Sarah was again overcome with grief, and on the advice
15 of a friend visited a fortune-teller. The fortune-teller told her that her bad luck was being caused by the ghosts of all the people who had been killed by the Winchester Rifle. The fortune-teller also told her to sell her home and "head towards the setting sun." Sarah Winchester took the fortune-teller's advice and moved west to California, where she found the perfect house for her.

20 The original house was a six-room farmhouse. As soon as she arrived, Sarah started taking the fortune-teller's second piece of advice. She was told to never stop building her house. Using the money her husband had left her, she employed over twenty builders who worked night and day on the house. Every morning, Sarah would meet the foreman[1] of the builders and give him hand-drawn building
25 plans for the day. This went on until Sarah's death in 1921.

Today, the house has over 160 rooms, 13 bathrooms, 47 fireplaces, 40 staircases, and three elevators. Guests at the house can look out over the land around the Winchester house from any of the house's 10,000 windows. It is also easy for guests to get lost in the house. There are also, by some estimates, 2,000 doors if
30 you include all the closets in the Winchester house, and doors behind which guests can find nothing but walls! Dozens of secret halls and trap doors[2] are also built into the house. The reason why Sarah Winchester made all these changes isn't entirely known. Many people think it was to **confuse** the many ghosts who are said to **haunt** the house. Others think that Sarah was simply **insane**. Either
35 way, Winchester House is now a major tourist attraction and brings in thousands of visitors a year.

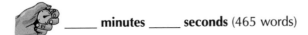 _____ **minutes** _____ **seconds** (465 words)

---

[1] **foreman** the person who manages a group of workers
[2] **trap door** a small flat door in a floor or ceiling

Reading Comprehension

Circle the letter of the best answer.

1. What is the best title for this passage?
   - **a.** The History of the Winchester Rifle
   - **b.** A Sad Childhood
   - **c.** The Story of a Remarkable House
   - **d.** The Life of William Winchester

2. What was Sarah's relationship to Oliver?
   - **a.** daughter
   - **b.** daughter-in-law
   - **c.** wife
   - **d.** mother

3. Who designed Winchester House?
   - **a.** William Winchester
   - **b.** a fortune-teller
   - **c.** a foreman
   - **d.** Sarah Winchester

4. Which statement about William Winchester is true?
   - **a.** He invented the Winchester Rifle.
   - **b.** He lived in Winchester House.
   - **c.** He was killed by a Winchester Rifle.
   - **d.** His wife was his heir.

5. Which statement about Sarah Winchester is NOT true?
   - **a.** She is thought by some people to have been insane.
   - **b.** She died thirty years after her husband.
   - **c.** She built a house which contained 2,000 doors.
   - **d.** She inherited a fortune.

Idioms

Find each idiom in the story.

1. **give/take advice**—*tell/listen to information given as help*
   - She always **gave** her younger sister **advice** about boys.
   - Frances hates to **take advice**. She prefers to work things out for herself.

2. **get lost**—*not know where one is; become unable to find the correct direction*
   - Nancy **got lost** in a shopping center when she was young.
   - Hold hands with one another, children. I don't want anyone to **get lost**.

3. **go on**—*continue*
   - The war **went on** for many years.
   - He starred in his first movie at the age of sixteen, and then **went on** to win several awards for his acting.

Vocabulary Reinforcement

A. Circle the letter of the word or phrase that best completes the sentence.

1. At the airport, luggage is checked for knives and other _____.

   a. damages   **b.** rifles   **c.** weapons   **d.** disasters

2. I'm _____. I don't understand what you want me to do.

   a. confused   **b.** accessible   **c.** insane   **d.** haunted

3. The wedding cake had been _____ by a professional, and was beautiful.

   a. injected   **b.** confused   **c.** participated   **d.** decorated

4. Some people think that old house is _____ by the ghost of the previous owner.

   a. haunted   **b.** inherited   **c.** insane   **d.** ruined

5. The sinking of the *Titanic* was a _____.

   a. harm   **b.** tragedy   **c.** grief   **d.** leak

6. Several years ago Michael Jackson bought the _____ for many of the Beatles' songs.

   a. rights   **b.** promotes   **c.** episodes   **d.** profits

7. Despite leaving university before he graduated, he _____ to become one of the richest men in the country.

   a. ended up   **b.** went on   **c.** moved on   **d.** cashed in on

8. After the old woman died, her _____ argued over her will.

   a. community   **b.** rights   **c.** inherits   **d.** heirs

B. Complete the passage with items from the box. One item is extra.

grief	haunted	insane	rifles	took the advice	confusing	get lost

The Winchester house was rebuilt by Sarah Winchester, a very rich woman who might have been (1)_____. After her daughter and husband died, Mrs. Winchester was overcome with (2)_____ and tried to get help from a fortune-teller. The fortune-teller told her that her bad luck came from the ghosts of all the people killed by Winchester (3)_____. The fortune-teller advised her to move west and rebuild her house constantly. She (4)_____ and made a house so big and (5)_____ that both people and ghosts could (6)_____ walking around inside of it.

What Do You Think?

1. What do you think was the reason for the strange design of Sarah's house?
2. If you were designing your dream house, what would it look like? What would it include?

Before You Read

Answer the following questions.

1. Do you ever watch or play baseball?

   _____

   _____

2. How popular is baseball in your country?

   _____

   _____

3. Do you know of any baseball players from your country who play abroad?

   _____

   _____

Target Vocabulary

Match each word with the best meaning.

1. _____ be accustomed to
2. _____ contract
3. _____ count
4. _____ diversity
5. _____ instructor
6. _____ (to) pitch
7. _____ proud
8. _____ recall
9. _____ recruit
10. _____ (to) face

a. pleased or satisfied with an achievement

b. a written and signed agreement

c. a teacher

d. variety

e. be important; matter

f. be used to something

g. meet with courage

h. interview and choose people to join a group or company

i. remember

j. throw a ball in baseball

Filipe Alou has watched the faces of baseball change a lot since he first started playing in the U.S. Major League[1] in the 1950s. At that time, he was the one of the first Major League players from a Spanish-speaking country. Now in his sixties, Alou is a Major League manager. As he watches international players from his own
5 country, the Dominican Republic, play on teams with players from Puerto Rico, Cuba, Venezuela, Japan, and Korea, he **recalls** the tough years he had in the past. And he'll **proudly** tell anyone, "We were the ones who opened the doors for the rest of them."

Searching for new young baseball players with potential, team **recruiters** these
10 days are traveling all around the world. In 2003, about one in every four players on Major League teams in the United States came from a foreign country, including players from South America, Asia, Europe, Australia, Canada, and the Caribbean. And in the minor leagues, almost half of the players with professional **contracts** were born outside the United States.

15 Probably the most internationally mixed team in either the U.S. American League or National League (the two professional baseball leagues in the United States) is the Montreal Expos. Among the forty players on the team, ten different countries are represented. During practice one day, one of the team's **pitching instructors**, Claude Raymond, recalled, "We were on the mound[2] talking about situations pitchers could
20 **face** and we had a Korean, a Japanese, a Dominican, a Mexican, a French-Canadian, a white American, and a black American all there." This comes as no surprise to fans of the team. They say their city has always welcomed **diversity**.

Although diversity is important, what really **counts** is performance, and international players of the past have just gone to show that great baseball players
25 don't have to be American. From Puerto Rico came Roberto Clemente, who became the first Latin American to be voted into the National Baseball Hall of Fame.[3] He played in the major leagues from 1955 until his death in 1972. Another Latin player who made it into the Hall of Fame is Luis Aparicio from Venezuela, who played in the majors from 1956 to 1973. Both of these players have been listed
30 among the top 100 baseball players of all time.

These days fans are **accustomed** to seeing talented players coming from Asian countries including Korea, the Philippines, and Japan. Japanese players have been recruited by Major League teams since the 1960s, but few of those players were able to make big names for themselves, at least not until 2001. That year Ichiro
35 Suzuki caught the attention of baseball fans everywhere. It was his first year playing on a Major League team, and he got 242 hits, stole 56 bases, and helped lead his team to 116 wins for the year. Suzuki was named the American League Rookie[4] of the Year and also Most Valuable Player of the Year for the American League.

_____ **minutes** _____ **seconds** (495 words)

---

[1] **Major League** professional baseball of the highest level
[2] **the mound** the place in a baseball diamond where the pitcher throws the ball from
[3] **Hall of Fame** a baseball museum where the best players are honored
[4] **rookie** new player

Reading Comprehension

Circle the letter of the best answer.

1. Where is Filipe Alou from?

   a. Spain

   b. the United States

   c. the Dominican Republic

   d. Puerto Rico

2. Which of the following statements is true?

   a. Major League teams have more foreign-born players than Minor League teams.

   b. So far, no foreign-born players are in the Hall of Fame.

   c. Major League teams have only started recruiting Asian players within the last ten years.

   d. Fans are now used to foreign-born players on Major League teams.

3. According to the passage, which place has always welcomed diversity?

   a. the United States

   b. Montreal

   c. the Dominican Republic

   d. Mexico

4. How many nationalities does Claude Raymond remember talking to one day?

   a. five

   b. six

   c. seven

   d. eight

5. Which of these players has NOT received an award?

   a. Luis Aparicio

   b. Roberto Clemente

   c. Ichiro Suzuki

   d. Filipe Alou

Idioms

Find each idiom in the story.

1. **come as a surprise**—*be surprising; happen without warning*
   - The extra money for his work **came as a** complete **surprise** to him.
   - This may **come as a surprise** to you, but English is not my first language.

2. **make a name (for oneself)**—*become well-known for something; become famous in one's occupation*
   - She **made a name for herself** in politics by running for mayor.
   - You'll never **make a name for yourself** in sales. Maybe you should change your career.

3. **(just) go to show**—*prove that something is true or is the case in the end*
   - Only half of the people on the boat survived the journey, which **just goes to show** how dangerous sea trips were at that time.
   - We both got good grades in the class. That **goes to show** how useful our study group was.

Vocabulary Reinforcement

A. Circle the letter of the word or phrase that best completes the sentence.

1. I thought we were friends, so her reaction _____.

   a. argued   **b.** was accustomed   **c.** was shocked   **d.** came as a surprise

2. After Becky's husband lost his job, she could no longer live as comfortably as she was _____.

   a. used   **b.** accustomed to   **c.** recalled   **d.** decorated

3. In his life, he has _____ many problems, but has overcome them all.

   a. faced   **b.** moved on   **c.** counted   **d.** taken advice on

4. This has been the hottest summer that anyone can _____.

   a. recall   **b.** count   **c.** promote   **d.** establish

5. After she retired from dancing professionally, she got work as a dance _____.

   a. heir   **b.** pitcher   **c.** instructor   **d.** contract

6. In my opinion, attitude _____ more than ability.

   a. promotes   **b.** counts   **c.** harms   **d.** is accustomed to

7. Janine was so _____ when her daughter graduated from college.

   a. holy   **b.** proud   **c.** grieved   **d.** tough

8. I don't believe you. What you say just doesn't _____.

   a. make sense   **b.** make an impression   **c.** confuse   **d.** come as a surprise

B. Complete the passage with items from the box. One item is extra.

contracts	proud	goes to show	diversity	recruiting	made a name	pitcher

American Major League baseball has more (1)_____ today than in the past. Major League teams are now (2)_____ players from around the world. And there are even more international players in the minor leagues. In the minors, about half of the players who have signed professional (3)_____ come from countries outside the United States. In fact, two players from Spanish-speaking countries were named in the top 100 players of all time, and recently one (4)_____ from Japan (5)_____ for himself as Rookie of the Year in his first year in the league. That just (6)_____ that great baseball players don't have to be born in the United States.

What Do You Think?

1. Are there any foreign-born athletes playing sports in your country? Why do they play there?
2. What are the pros and cons of a country using foreign-born athletes?

Strange Foods 15

Before You Read

Answer the following questions.

1. There is an English saying, "One man's meat is another man's poison." What do you think it means? Do you agree?

_____

_____

2. What is the strangest food you have ever eaten?

_____

_____

3. Are there any foods in your country that visitors from another country might find strange?

_____

_____

Target Vocabulary

Match each word with the best meaning.

1. _____ boil
2. _____ disgusting
3. _____ entire
4. _____ feast
5. _____ fry
6. _____ insect
7. _____ resemble
8. _____ stomach
9. _____ (to) stuff
10. _____ tribe

a. fill something by tightly pushing other things into it
b. complete; whole
c. the part of an animal's body where food goes after it is swallowed
d. cook in hot water (at 100°C)
e. a large meal with many dishes
f. cook in hot oil
g. a small animal with six legs and three body parts
h. look like
i. causing strong dislike; offensive; making one sick
j. a group of people with the same language and culture who live together (often in villages)

"Yuck! What is that? I'm not going to eat that!" Have you heard these words before? You've probably even said them or thought them yourself at some time. We all have different tastes for foods we like or don't like. Some people hate anchovies.[1] Other people love them. Some people would never consider eating

5 bugs.[2] For other people, **insects** are a normal part of their diet. A lot of what certain people choose to eat depends on the culture in which they are raised.

One interesting food that is eaten by some people in Australia is grilled crocodile. To make this dish, people use the meat from a crocodile's tail. A nice steak cut from the tail can be grilled just like beef. Some people say crocodile meat tastes

10 like a cross between pork and chicken. Other people compare it to veal.[3] Crocodile meat can also be used to make sausage.

Few people in Scotland have ever tried crocodile sausage, and most probably wouldn't be interested in trying it even if they could. On the other hand, haggis makes a tasty dinner in Scotland. Haggis, which **resembles** a large sausage, is

15 made from a sheep's **stomach** that has been **stuffed** with the sheep's other organs like the lungs, liver, and heart. The recipe also calls for oatmeal and spices, which are mixed with the organs before putting them into the stomach. The stuffed stomach is then **boiled** and served with "neeps and tatties," mashed turnips[4] and potatoes. Haggis is a very special dish in Scotland, traditionally served on special

20 days like Robbie Burns Day (January 25), the day celebrating the birthday of Scotland's national poet.

Like haggis, many other interesting foods around the world are only prepared on special occasions. In the Middle East and some parts of North Africa, members of the Bedouin[5] **tribe** may prepare roasted camel as a special **feast** to serve at

25 wedding celebrations. This food is not easy to prepare, but when people want to go all out for a wedding, they ask the whole tribe to help with the effort. Tribe members first cook an egg mixture which they put inside cooked fish. These fish are then put inside several cooked chickens. The chickens are then put into roasted sheep. Usually one or two sheep will be enough to fill one roasted camel.

30 One roasted camel serves twenty or thirty people, so this dish may be enjoyed by the **entire** tribe at the wedding.

To many Americans, grilled crocodile, haggis, and roasted camel may seem very strange. People might even say these foods are **disgusting**. But some things many Americans enjoy, such as **fried** cheese and even fried ice cream, may seem strange

35 or disgusting to other cultures, too. As the old saying says, "to each his own."

 _____ **minutes** _____ **seconds** (464 words)

---

[1] **anchovy** a small fish that is often salted
[2] **bug** an insect, especially a beetle
[3] **veal** meat from a young cow
[4] **mashed turnips** turnips (an underground vegetable) that have been crushed until soft
[5] **Bedouin** an Arab tribe

Reading Comprehension

Circle the letter of the best answer.

1. According to the passage, grilled crocodile does NOT taste like . . .

   a. beef.

   b. pork.

   c. veal.

   d. chicken.

2. Which of the meals mentioned in the passage would a vegetarian most enjoy?

   a. haggis

   b. a Bedouin feast

   c. neeps and tatties

   d. the Australian grill

3. In what way are haggis and the Bedouin feast similar?

   a. They are both boiled.

   b. They both involve stuffing food.

   c. They are both usually eaten at weddings.

   d. They are both made from meat from several different animals.

4. The Bedouin feast is . . .

   a. usually fried.

   b. prepared by one or two people.

   c. only prepared on special occasions.

   d. made with oatmeal and spices.

5. The main idea of the passage is . . .

   a. a lot of the food in Australia and Scotland is very unusual.

   b. all cultures eat food that some other cultures find strange.

   c. you should try food from many different cultures.

   d. most cultures find food from other cultures disgusting.

Idioms

Find each idiom in the story.

1. **a cross between (something and something)**—*not one thing or the other, but a mixture of both*
   - **A cross between** a lion and a female tiger is called a *liger*.
   - That flower looks like **a cross between** a rose and a tulip.

2. **call for**—*need; require*
   - The situation **called for** quick action.
   - How much butter does the recipe **call for**?

3. **go all out**—*use all energy or resources to do something special*
   - The Andersons really **went all out** for the party.
   - Cathy **went all out** for her date. She bought a new dress and got a new haircut.

Vocabulary Reinforcement

A. Circle the letter of the word or phrase that best completes the sentence.

1. I really couldn't eat another thing; my _____ is too full.
   a. stuffed **b.** stomach **c.** feast **d.** dish

2. One way to make polluted water drinkable is to _____ it for ten minutes.
   a. fry **b.** grill **c.** boil **d.** roast

3. Many people incorrectly think that spiders are _____.
   a. insects **b.** animals **c.** architects **d.** webs

4. Eating food you find on the ground is _____.
   a. a feast **b.** spectacular **c.** delicious **d.** disgusting

5. After the festival, the whole village sat down to eat a(n) _____.
   a. feast **b.** anchovy **c.** insect **d.** empire

6. If you are on a diet you shouldn't eat too many _____ foods.
   a. boiled **b.** fried **c.** grilled **d.** roasted

7. Jack and his brother don't really _____ each other.
   a. cross between **b.** tell apart **c.** resemble **d.** face

8. The story is _____ a romance and a ghost story.
   a. resemble **b.** written **c.** accustomed to **d.** a cross between

B. Complete the passage with items from the box. One item is extra.

calls for	goes all out	fries	stuffed	resembles	tribe	entire

Here are two examples of special foods eaten in two very different cultures. In Scotland, there is a famous dish called haggis, which (1)_____ a large sausage. The recipe for haggis not only (2)_____ sheep's stomach, but also for other organs like the lungs, heart, and liver. When a Bedouin tribe (3)_____ to celebrate a wedding, they might serve a(n) (4)_____ roasted camel (5)_____ with fish, chickens, and sheep. This dish can serve a(n) (6)_____ of thirty people.

What Do You Think?

1. Which of the dishes in the passage would you most like to try? Which would you least like to try?

2. Imagine you were organizing a big feast. What would you serve?

A. Circle the correct answer for each question.

1. You are more likely to be jealous of someone _____.   **a.** rich   **b.** poor
2. Which do many people decorate at Christmas time?   **a.** a feast   **b.** a tree
3. Which are people more accustomed to?   **a.** spending money   **b.** receiving awards
4. Which of these is a weapon?   **a.** an empire   **b.** a rifle
5. Which of these flows?   **a.** water   **b.** an insect
6. When can you make an impression?   **a.** at a meeting   **b.** in the kitchen
7. Which would people rather feel?   **a.** pride   **b.** grief
8. Which would you invite friends to share with you?   **a.** a contract   **b.** a feast
9. Which would you sign?   **a.** a recruit   **b.** a contract
10. Which movie would be enjoyed by fewer people?   **a.** conventional   **b.** alternative

B. Complete the paragraph with items from the box. Two items are extra.

came as a surprise	community	establishing	faced	grief	heir
made a name for	pressure	rights	took over	weapons	resembled

Many people change countries during their life, but one man has (1)_____ himself by (2)_____ his own country. During World War II, England built a number of artificial platforms off the coast of England to contain (3)_____ to fight off invaders. After the war, the soldiers left these platforms and they were forgotten—until 1967. In that year, a British man, Roy Bates, (4)_____ one of the platforms and announced he had started his own country, called Sealand.

This (5)_____ to England, who believed they had the (6)_____ to the platform. Bates, who renamed himself Prince Roy, and the small (7)_____ on the island (his family), (8)_____ a great deal of (9)_____ from England to leave the platform. However, in 1968 an English court decided that because Sealand was over ten kilometers off the English coast, it was in international waters, and England had no power there. Today, Sealand, which even has its own stamps, coins, and passports, is controlled by Roy's son and (10)_____, Prince Michael, and is home to a large Internet business.

C. Circle the odd one out in each group.

1. **a.** insane   **b.** mentally ill   **c.** abnormal   **d.** average
2. **a.** tragedy   **b.** grief   **c.** happiness   **d.** disaster
3. **a.** tribe   **b.** individual   **c.** gang   **d.** team
4. **a.** one another   **b.** solitary   **c.** together   **d.** each other
5. **a.** impression   **b.** attitude   **c.** feeling   **d.** factor
6. **a.** fry   **b.** feast   **c.** grill   **d.** boil
7. **a.** gun   **b.** rifle   **c.** knife   **d.** insect
8. **a.** knee   **b.** brain   **c.** lung   **d.** stomach
9. **a.** entire   **b.** to an extent   **c.** complete   **d.** whole
10. **a.** come to an end   **b.** move on   **c.** continue   **d.** go on

D. Use the clues below to complete the crossword.

Across

1. The British _____ was once the largest in the world.
3. The whole _____ live together in the village.
6. The _____ of the award was very happy.
8. Next lesson we'll _____ to the next chapter. (2 words)
10. Sometimes olives are _____ with anchovies.
13. She was put into the mental hospital for being _____.
15. After his wife died, his _____ was terrible.
16. Every morning I _____ the job section in the newspaper.
18. A police officer often has to _____ difficult situations.
19. I don't know who did it, but I _____ to find out.

11. Cultural _____ is increasing as more people come from other countries.
12. Hard work is the _____ to success.
14. To make chips, _____ potatoes in hot oil.
17. He left all his money to his _____, his daughter.

Down

1. start; found
2. This shirt is too small. Can I _____ it for a bigger one?
4. If you leave your bicycle in the rain, you'll _____ it.
5. He was so hungry he ate the _____ cake.
7. I'm _____. Can you explain this to me?
9. That meal was _____. I feel sick.

Secret Stations 16

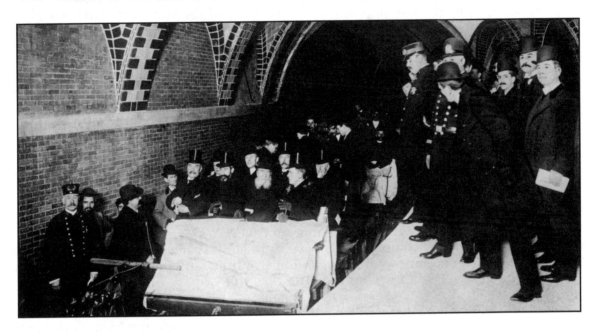

Before You Read

Answer the following questions.

1. Look at the photograph. Where do you think this is? When do you think the photo was taken? _____

2. Which places in your country have a subway system? Which ones have you been on? _____

3. Do you think there are any subway lines or stations in your country that are no longer in use? _____

Target Vocabulary

Match each word with the best meaning.

1. _____ abandoned
2. _____ curved
3. _____ facilities
4. _____ landmark
5. _____ passenger
6. _____ renovate
7. _____ reserve
8. _____ schedule
9. _____ suspend
10. _____ tiles

a. stop something for a period of time

b. empty; left behind; no longer used

c. a person (not the driver) who rides in a plane, bus, taxi, car, etc.

d. bent; not straight

e. make an older building look like new

f. a list of timed, planned activities or events

g. thin plates of clay, or stone put down to cover a floor or walls

h. an easily seen building, or a historical building or point of interest

i. services, including the rooms, etc., provided by an organization

j. save a place in a hotel room, on an airplane, on a tour, etc.

71

New York Transit Museum: Ghost Station Tour
City Hall Station, an **abandoned** station of the New York Rapid Transit subway, was originally the last stop at the southern end of the subway's interborough[1] line. The station opened in 1904, and was designed to be the most impressive station
5 of the city's new subway system.

City Hall Station remained in use until 1945, when the station had to be closed due to certain changes in the city's subway system. As more and more **passengers** started to travel by subway, it became necessary to add more cars to subway trains. This meant that subway platforms needed to be extended to fit the longer
10 trains. However, City Hall Station was originally built with a short, **curved** platform, making **renovations** to the station difficult. Rather than trying to rebuild it, officials chose to abandon City Hall Station in favor of another nearby station, the Brooklyn Bridge Station. Apart from being easier to renovate, the Brooklyn Bridge Station was also used by more passengers each day than City
15 Hall Station. In its final year, City Hall Station was used by only six hundred passengers a day, a very small number for New York City. Thus, City Hall became a "ghost" station on the New York subway line, a modern underground ruin. Today, one subway line, the Number 6 train, still passes through City Hall Station on its way north, but the train does not stop.

20 In 1998, the New York Transit Museum reopened City Hall Station for tourists. Due to the historic significance and beauty of this station, the New York Transit Museum **schedules** special tours of the station several times each year. A few of the features guests will notice in this unique station include the arches and skylight[2] built above the platform, the colored glass **tiles** decorating the walls, and
25 brass chandeliers[3] hanging from the ceiling. The station has also been named as a **landmark** by the U.S. government.

Tour Information and Reservations
Please make **reservations** with the Transit Museum from Tuesday to Friday, 10 A.M. to 4 P.M. Payment in advance is required for tours and must be received at
30 least one week before the scheduled tour. Payment can be made by credit card or check.

Tours may require a lot of walking. Wear good walking shoes and comfortable clothes. For your safety, follow the instructions of the tour guide when touring abandoned stations, stay with the group at all times, and otherwise follow
35 instructions or signs at the **facilities**.

Photography is not permitted inside abandoned facilities.

Note: Tours of City Hall Station have been **suspended** *as of 2001 due to increased security citywide in New York.*

_____ **minutes** _____ **seconds** (451 words)

---

[1] **interborough** the prefix "inter-" means "between." There are five boroughs (areas) in New York City: Manhattan, Queens, the Bronx, Brooklyn, and Staten Island.
[2] **skylight** a window in the ceiling
[3] **chandelier** a decorative frame that holds lights and hangs from the ceiling

Reading Comprehension

Circle the letter of the best answer.

1. Which sentence about this subway station is true?

   a. It is said to be haunted by a ghost.

   b. It is a government secret.

   c. It is no longer being used.

   d. It was first used in 1945.

2. What made renovation of the station difficult?

   a. people not using the station

   b. the size of the tracks

   c. passengers from the Brooklyn Bridge Station

   d. the way the platform was built

3. How often were scheduled tours of the station held?

   a. several times a day

   b. once a day

   c. a few times each week

   d. less than once a month

4. Which would visitors to the station NOT see?

   a. chandeliers

   b. decorated walls

   c. passengers

   d. sunlight

5. Which statement about the tours is true today?

   a. Tour guides walk with visitors.

   b. Tours require a reservation.

   c. Tours are no longer offered.

   d. Tours can be reserved up to a week in advance.

Idioms

Find each idiom in the story.

1. **in favor of**—*on the side of; in support of*
   - Everyone was **in favor of** taking a break.
   - Many people are **in favor of** higher taxes to support more government programs.

2. **in advance**—*before a particular date or event*
   - You can get a discount if you pay for the event **in advance**.
   - Tickets for the concert need to be bought at least two weeks **in advance**.

3. **as of (a date or time)**—*from a particular date or time*
   - **As of** September 1st, ticket prices for the museum will increase to $6.
   - **As of** yesterday, she is no longer a student. She graduated.

Vocabulary Reinforcement

A. Circle the letter of the word or phrase that best completes the sentence.

1. The boy was _____ from school for smoking in class.
   a. curved   **b.** suspended   **c.** abandoned   **d.** scheduled

2. A good example of a famous *landmark* is _____.
   a. Australia   **b.** Elvis Presley   **c.** the Eiffel Tower   **d.** the sun

3. Although the hotel isn't in the best location, it has great _____.
   a. facilities   **b.** passengers   **c.** guests   **d.** reservations

4. The office will be closed down _____ the end of next month.
   a. as for   **b.** as of   **c.** in advance   **d.** as well as

5. If you can't come to my party, please let me know _____.
   a. reserved   **b.** as of   **c.** by and large   **d.** in advance

6. The bus can take a driver and thirty _____.
   a. guests   **b.** facilities   **c.** passengers   **d.** reservations

7. Can you look at the movie _____ and tell me what time that film is on?
   a. reservation   **b.** schedule   **c.** contract   **d.** impression

8. An example of a *curved* object is _____.
   a. a banana   **b.** a knife   **c.** a diamond   **d.** a steak

B. Complete the passage with items from the box. One item is extra.

abandoned	in favor of	renovated	reserved	suspended	tiles	landmark

City Hall Station in New York is no longer in use and is one of the city's (1)_____ subway stations. The station, which is now a historic (2)_____, was built with many unique features such as glass (3)_____ on the walls, brass chandeliers, and a skylight. However, when the subway lines were being (4)_____, subway officials voted (5)_____ closing City Hall and putting more effort toward fixing the nearby Brooklyn Bridge Station. The Transit Museum in New York offered tours of City Hall Station for a few years, but the tours have been (6)_____ as of 2001.

What Do You Think?

1. Would you like to go on this tour? Why or why not?

2. This tour has been suspended because of security concerns in New York. Is your country worried about security? Have any security-related changes taken place in recent years? If yes, what kind of changes have taken place?

Taekwondo

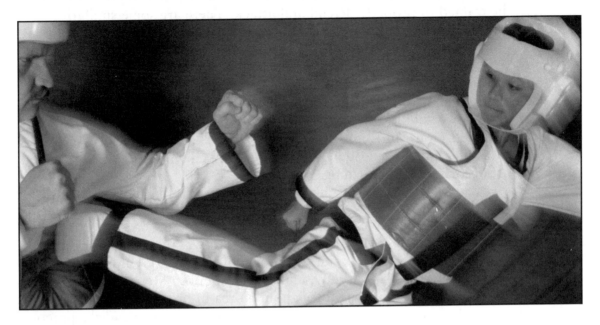

Before You Read

Answer the following questions.

1. What martial arts do you know? Which are popular in your country?

2. What do you know about the history of these martial arts? Where do they come from?

3. What do you know about taekwondo? What do you think "taekwondo" means?

Target Vocabulary

Match each word with the best meaning.

1. _____ authorities   **a.** people in power; the government

2. _____ combat   **b.** protect against attack

3. _____ defend   **c.** show where or what something is

4. _____ ethics   **d.** area

5. _____ indicate   **e.** a weapon with a handle and a long steel blade

6. _____ philosophy   **f.** the study of questions about what is right and wrong to do

7. _____ region   **g.** a violent fight

8. _____ sword   **h.** a fighter; a soldier

9. _____ tomb   **i.** a burial room or grave with a monument over it

10. _____ warrior   **j.** the study of general truths and beliefs of humans, the world, and life

Reading Passage Track 17

Taekwondo is the Korean martial art[1] of hand-to-hand **combat**. Perhaps that should really be body-to-body combat, because in taekwondo the whole body must be trained to properly **defend** and attack. There are some similarities between taekwondo and other martial arts, such as karate and judo, but there are
5 several important differences. For example, taekwondo uses quick, straight-line moves, like those which can also be found in Japanese martial arts, but taekwondo also uses flowing circular moves like the type of moves found in Chinese martial arts. The main difference between taekwondo and other martial arts is the powerful kicking technique which taekwondo uses, and which gives
10 taekwondo its name. In Korean, *tae* means "to kick," *kwon* means "to strike with the hand," and *do* means "art." Therefore, taekwondo can be translated as "the art of kicking and punching."

Paintings found in ancient Korean **tombs indicate** that a martial art similar to taekwondo has been practiced in Korea since about 50 B.C. Also, records of a
15 specially trained group of young **warriors** called Hwarang explain how these young men were taught *subak* (an early form of taekwondo) along with history, **philosophy, ethics**, archery,[2] riding, and **sword** fighting. Members of the Hwarang were also encouraged to travel throughout Korea in order to learn about the people who lived in all **regions** of the country. This helped spread the practice of
20 subak throughout Korea. Eventually, subak, which was practiced for exercise and sport, gave way to *taek kyon*, which expanded on subak by focusing more on the feet and kicking. The purpose of taek kyon was specifically fighting, so members of the military were required to learn it. However, over time, people's interest in taek kyon and subak died out. By the 1800s, few Koreans actually practiced
25 either.

After Korea was invaded in 1909, **authorities** put an end to the practice of all martial arts in the country. In the long run, this ban actually led to increased interest in martial arts, and secret groups began to practice subak and taek kyon again in the Buddhist temples hidden high in the mountains in Korea. After Korea
30 gained its independence again in 1948, interest in many forms of martial arts grew around the country. In 1955, a group of top Korean martial artists chose taekwondo as an official martial art, and in 1971 the Korean president, Park Chung Hee, declared taekwondo as the national sport of Korea.

Today, taekwondo enjoys great popularity around the world. More than 20
35 million people practice taekwondo in more than 120 countries. Taekwondo was made an official Olympic sport at the 2000 Olympic Games in Sydney.

 _____ **minutes** _____ **seconds** (437 words)

---

[1] **martial art** a self-defense technique, such as judo, karate, aikido, taekwondo, kung fu
[2] **archery** a sport in which people shoot arrows at a target, using a bow

Reading Comprehension

Circle the letter of the best answer.

1. The Korean martial arts in this passage, from oldest to newest are . . .

   a. subak, taek kyon, taekwondo.

   b. taekwondo, subak, taek kyon.

   c. taek kyon, subak, taekwondo.

   d. taekwondo, taek kyon, subak.

2. When was taekwondo recognized as a martial art?

   a. 50 B.C.

   b. 1955

   c. 1971

   d. 2000

3. What is the main difference between taekwondo and other martial arts?

   a. the punching techniques

   b. the kicking techniques

   c. the quick, straight lines of the techniques

   d. the flowing, circular moves of the techniques

4. Which statement about taekwondo is NOT true?

   a. It was banned until 1971.

   b. It has a two-thousand-year-old history.

   c. It is now practiced all around the world.

   d. It can be used to both defend and attack.

5. Which martial art does modern taekwondo most resemble?

   a. subak

   b. taek kyon

   c. karate

   d. judo

Idioms

Find each idiom in the story.

1. **put an end to**—*stop*
   - We need to **put an end to** all of this fighting.
   - Mary **put an end to** the party at midnight, and told everyone to leave.

2. **die out**—*slowly disappear*
   - The noise **died out** as the train moved away.
   - All of the fish will **die out** if the factory goes on spilling pollution into the lake.

3. **give way to**—*end so that something else can begin*
   - As temperatures increased, the grass eventually **gave way to** desert.
   - Disco gradually died out and **gave way to** other types of music.

Vocabulary Reinforcement

A. Circle the letter of the word or phrase that best completes the sentence.

1. *Tombs* are made to contain _____.
   a. dead people   **b.** passengers   **c.** office workers   **d.** food

2. The list on the wall _____ which classroom each student should be in.
   a. suggests   **b.** indicates   **c.** ethics   **d.** reserves

3. Accidentally killing someone while trying to _____ yourself isn't usually considered murder.
   a. attack   **b.** combat   **c.** put an end to   **d.** defend

4. Most journalists and lawyers have to study _____ at university.
   a. ethics   **b.** combat   **c.** authorities   **d.** facilities

5. My grandfather was awarded a medal for brave _____ in World War II.
   a. warrior   **b.** weapons   **c.** martial arts   **d.** combat

6. Be careful with that _____. It is not a toy.
   a. insect   **b.** sword   **c.** warrior   **d.** tomb

7. I've had enough of my neighbor. I'm going to _____ their noisy parties right now.
   a. put an end to   **b.** give way to   **c.** combat   **d.** die out

8. The _____ have decided to hold an election next year.
   a. facilities   **b.** warriors   **c.** authorities   **d.** regions

B. Complete the passage with items from the box. One item is extra.

authorities	warriors	died out	ethics	gave way to	regions	philosophy

Taekwondo is a kind of martial art that originated in Korea. A long time ago, students were taught an early form of taekwondo in school along with other courses like (1)_____, ethics, and history. As these student (2)_____ traveled through various (3)_____ of the country, they spread this kind of martial art. Over time, this original kind of taekwondo (4)_____ a form which had a stronger focus on combat than exercise. However, interest in both of these early martial arts (5)_____ over time. It was not until the twentieth century that interest in taekwondo really grew again, and eventually (6)_____ in Korea named it the national sport.

What Do You Think?

1. What skills do you think someone needs to become a good martial artist?

2. Are there any other sports that you think should become official Olympic sports? Why?

White Sands

▊ Before You Read

Answer the following questions.

1. Look at the photograph. Where do you think this is? How would you describe this place?

_____

_____

2. Are there any deserts or dry places in your country? If not, what countries have deserts?

_____

_____

3. What places are popular for hiking in your country?

_____

_____

▊ Target Vocabulary

Match each word with the best meaning.

1. _____ (to) alternate   **a.** turn; curve

2. _____ blind   **b.** unable to see

3. _____ brochure   **c.** move smoothly over a surface

4. _____ crystal   **d.** a path for hiking or horse riding

5. _____ dissolve   **e.** change from a liquid to a gas as temperature increases

6. _____ evaporate   **f.** mix something in a liquid so it disappears

7. _____ mineral   **g.** change back and forth between one thing and another

8. _____ slide   **h.** a thin printed book describing a company's products or services

9. _____ (to) wind   **i.** a substance found naturally in the earth, such as iron, tin, copper

10. _____ trail   **j.** a small piece of a substance that has formed naturally into a regular shape

At the entrance to White Sands National Monument, a narrow road begins to **wind** its way through large rolling white hills. One might think these hills were covered with snow except for the fact that it is over thirty degrees[1] outside. No, this is not snow. These hills are covered with bright white sand, gypsum[2] **crystals**
5 really. Under the midday sun, the white sand is **blinding**. We have to put on our sunglasses before continuing our drive.

How did all of this white sand end up in a desert valley in southern New Mexico? It came from nearby Lake Lucero, just outside the park. Lake Lucero is actually a dry lake bed, but it may hold water from time to time during seasons with heavy
10 rain. Any water that collects in this lake bed is filled with **dissolved minerals**. When this water **evaporates**, gypsum crystals remain on the ground to be formed by **alternating** hot, cold, wet, and dry weather into sand.

It is hard to find this kind of sand in other parts of the world because gypsum dissolves easily in water. But because Lake Lucero is in the Chihuahuan Desert,
15 huge gypsum dunes have been able to form here. Over millions of years, the tiny bits of gypsum crystals have been blown by the wind and collected into a large desert of white sand dunes[3] that now covers more than 660,000 square kilometers.

We follow the blacktop road for 13 kilometers into the heart of the dunes. There,
20 the road ends in a parking lot surrounded on all sides by rolling white dunes. We watch other visitors to the park play in the dunes around the parking lot. Some have brought winter sleds and are **sliding** down the dunes on them. It looks like fun, but we decide it will be more fun to hike across the dunes. There are no real hiking **trails** in the park. The wind constantly blows the sand and wipes out all
25 trails and footprints[4] in a very short time. Instead of trails, the park management has put up bright orange poles for hikers to follow.

We decide to take the 11-kilometer-long Alkali Flat Trail. Before starting off on the trail, we have to sign a book to tell the park rangers how many people are in our group and the time we start our hike. When we finish hiking, we will sign the
30 book again to let them know we have returned. The park **brochure** says this trail will take us to the edge of the monument where the white sands end and the normal desert begins again.

As we set off across the gypsum dunes, we marvel at[5] the incredible scenery. Soon we lose sight of the parking lot, and all we can see is the blue sky above, the
35 brown mountains in the distance surrounding this desert valley, and white dunes all around. It looks like no other place on earth.

 _____ **minutes** _____ **seconds** (491 words)

---

[1] **thirty degrees** 30°C; thirty degrees Celsius
[2] **gypsum** a soft white mineral that looks like chalk
[3] **dune** a hill made of sand
[4] **footprint** the mark left on the ground by someone's foot
[5] **marvel at** to look at something with surprise, wonder, and admiration

Reading Comprehension

Circle the letter of the best answer.

1. Where might you find this reading?
   a. in a geography textbook
   b. in a national park brochure
   c. in a person's travel diary
   d. in an encyclopedia

2. Which is true about the white sand in this park?
   a. It is not really white.
   b. It is still forming today.
   c. It was formed by snow.
   d. It is evaporating over time.

3. Where is Lake Lucero?
   a. on a large dune
   b. in Mexico
   c. on a mountain
   d. outside the park

4. Which of the following would NOT be useful in the park?
   a. hiking boots
   b. sunglasses
   c. a sled
   d. a swimsuit

5. What is the book at the start of Alkali Flat Trail used for?
   a. to explain things hikers will see
   b. to help rangers protect the trail
   c. to record who is on the trail
   d. to show where the trail goes

Idioms

Find each idiom in the story.

1. **wipe out**—*completely erase*
   - The nuclear bomb test **wiped out** all life on the island.
   - This new cleaner will **wipe out** all the germs in your bathroom.

2. **set off**—*start a journey*
   - She **set off** early in the morning on her long drive across the country.
   - We will **set off** for the mountain at noon.

3. **put up**—*place something so that it's standing upright*
   - My grandfather **put up** the swing that is now hanging from the tree.
   - They plan to **put up** a fence to keep the cows from walking across the road.

Vocabulary Reinforcement

A. Circle the letter of the word or phrase that best completes the sentence.

1. My old watch doesn't use batteries. I need to _____ it every day.

    a. wind   **b.** wipe out   **c.** put up   **d.** slide

2. Sugar _____ when you put it into hot coffee.

    a. evaporates   **b.** dissolves   **c.** alternates   **d.** slides

3. I'm not sure where to go on vacation. I need to look through some _____.

    a. crystals   **b.** minerals   **c.** brochures   **d.** tombs

4. The fridge was too heavy to lift so I had to _____ it across the floor.

    a. wind   **b.** put up   **c.** slide   **d.** pitch

5. Salt and sugar form _____ naturally.

    a. crystals   **b.** minerals   **c.** alternatives   **d.** decorations

6. One family of cats managed to _____ all the birds on that island.

    a. call for   **b.** set off   **c.** come to an end   **d.** wipe out

7. Last weekend I helped my uncle _____ a fence on his farm.

    a. create   **b.** put up   **c.** establish   **d.** found

8. Michiko and Bill speak to each other in Japanese and English on _____ days.

    a. confusing   **b.** translating   **c.** alternating   **d.** scheduling

B. Complete the passage with items from the box. One item is extra.

alternating	blinding	evaporates	set off	wipes out	trails	mineral

White Sands is a national park where people can walk over large dunes of what looks like white sand. The sand is actually formed from crystals of gypsum, a kind of (1)_____. The sand forms in a dry lake bed near the park where rain water collects and then (2)_____. (3)_____ hot, cold, dry, and wet weather breaks the crystals into a fine powder. If you visit this park, be sure to bring sunglasses. The sunlight on the white sand can be (4)_____. And before you (5)_____ on any of the (6)_____ through the park, sign the guest book so the rangers know who is on the trail.

What Do You Think?

1. What adjectives does the writer use to describe White Sands?
Are there any places in your country that you could use these words to describe?

2. What place in your country "looks like no other place on earth?"

The Great Pretender

Before You Read

Answer the following questions.

1. Do you know any of the people pictured above? What do you know about them? _____

2. What books do you know that have been made into films? Is the story usually different between them? _____

3. How do you decide which books to read and which films to see? Do you usually read reviews? _____

Target Vocabulary

Match each word with the best meaning.

1. _____ available
2. _____ code
3. _____ dramatic
4. _____ fraud
5. _____ genius
6. _____ impersonate
7. _____ knowledge
8. _____ motive
9. _____ pretend
10. _____ reference

a. accessible; able to be had
b. exciting; happening suddenly; in a noticeable or surprising way
c. information about something
d. a mention of something
e. reason for doing something
f. a very intelligent person
g. to pass oneself off as someone else
h. to fake; act in a way that gives a false appearance
i. lying to someone to get their money or property
j. a series of symbols that have meaning; a way of writing a written message to make the meaning secret

83

He **pretended** to be a pilot and got free rides on international airlines to countries around the world. He wrote fake checks and stole several millions of dollars from banks, hotels, and airlines. He lied and got jobs by **impersonating** a doctor, a lawyer, and a university professor, all before he was twenty-one years old. Does
5   this sound like the story to movie? It is. But it is also true. This is the story of Frank Abagnale's life of crime told in Abagnale's book *Catch Me If You Can* and in the movie by the same name. Although the movie is based on the book, there are several important differences between the two.

Probably the one thing that really sets apart the book from the movie is the point-
10   of-view of the story. The book, co-written by Abagnale and a professional writer, is told in Abagnale's own words. In the book, he tells the reader, "I did this. This is how and this is why." But in the movie, the story is told from a third person's point-of-view. This point-of-view limits the details **available** to viewers of the movie.

15   Because the writer of the movie could not include many of the details about Abagnale's crimes and **motives**, the writer had to change things to make the story understandable for viewers. For example, Abagnale explains in the book how he used his **knowledge** of the banking system's number **codes** to commit **fraud**. In the movie, Abagnale has detailed knowledge of printing and check design, like a kind
20   of criminal **genius**. The movie's writer never tells the audience how Abagnale got all of this knowledge.

Another key difference between the book and movie has to do with the people trying to catch Abagnale. In the book, there are only a few **references** to an FBI[1] agent named O'Reilly, the man in charge of Abagnale's case. However, the movie
25   gives viewers a lot more information about how an FBI agent, renamed Hanratty, tracks down Abagnale and finally catches him.

There are a number of other major differences between the book and the movie about Abagnale's life, some which seem to make the book more interesting while others make the movie more interesting. In the end, it all comes down to the
30   question, "Which is better?" Like many other books that have been made into movies, the book is better in this case. The fictional parts of the movie may help create **dramatic** scenes for the movie and help viewers understand the story quickly, but they are fictional. There is an old saying, "Truth is stranger than fiction." And in this case, the truth is both stranger and more interesting.

_____ **minutes** _____ **seconds** (445 words)

---

[1] **FBI** Federal Bureau of Investigation, a United States government agency that is involved when national laws are broken or national security is threatened

Reading Comprehension

Circle the letter of the best answer.

1. Why is Frank Abagnale most famous?

   a. He directed a movie about his life.

   b. He stole a lot of money from the FBI.

   c. He talked his way into many different jobs.

   d. He was trained as a pilot, a lawyer, and a professor.

2. Which is true about the book and the movie?

   a. Both were not true.

   b. Neither was very popular.

   c. There are several major differences.

   d. They were written by the same person.

3. What did Abagnale know about in real life?

   a. how to fly a plane

   b. the number system used by banks

   c. directing movies

   d. working for the FBI

4. Who was O'Reilly?

   a. Abagnale's friend

   b. a writer helping Abagnale

   c. a man chasing Abagnale

   d. Hanratty's partner

5. Which of these sentences would the writer of this passage most likely agree with?

   a. The book is better than the film.

   b. The film is better than the book.

   c. The film and the book are equally good.

   d. None of the above.

Idioms

Find each idiom in the story.

1. **set apart**—*make different; put in a place to be separate from others*
   - How will you **set apart** the various plants you will grow in the garden?
   - His intelligence **sets** him **apart** from ordinary people.

2. **in charge of**—*having power over others; leading*
   - My mother is **in charge of** handling the money in our family's budget.
   - Who is **in charge of** the project?

3. **track down**—*hunt; search to find*
   - The dogs **tracked down** the rabbit to its hole.
   - The thief may try to hide, but the police will easily **track** her **down**.

Vocabulary Reinforcement

A. Circle the letter of the word or phrase that best completes the sentence.

1. Violet is a manager at the bank. She's _____ fifteen people.
   a. in charge of   **b.** impersonating   **c.** defending   **d.** tracking down

2. An old saying says, "_____ is power."
   a. fraud   **b.** knowledge   **c.** check   **d.** reference

3. To stop the enemy from reading it, the message was written in _____.
   a. drama   **b.** pretend   **c.** genius   **d.** code

4. Hurry! Buy now! This product is only _____ for a short time.
   a. available   **b.** in charge   **c.** indicated   **d.** counted

5. She was sent to prison for _____.
   a. genius   **b.** pretending   **c.** fraud   **d.** tracking down

6. The police are still trying to _____ the gang who robbed the bank.
   a. impersonate   **b.** track down   **c.** wipe out   **d.** give way to

7. Albert Einstein was one of the greatest _____ of the last century.
   a. geniuses   **b.** frauds   **c.** motives   **d.** warriors

8. In the last six months, the company has seen a _____ rise in profits.
   a. disappointing   **b.** pretend   **c.** disgusting   **d.** dramatic

B. Complete the passage with items from the box. One item is extra.

dramatic   impersonated   set apart   motive   reference   tracking down   pretending

Frank Abagnale was a young criminal who stole millions of dollars before he was twenty-one years old. He not only stole money, he (1)_____ professionals and got jobs working as a pilot, a professor, and a doctor. What was Abagnale's (2)_____ for (3)_____ to be these people? You can find the answer in the (4)_____ book he wrote about his life of crime. A movie has also been made about his life. The movie's writer and director make (5)_____ to the events in the book, but they also changed many things. These differences really (6)_____ the book and the movie.

What Do You Think?

1. Have you ever pretended to be something you're not? Why or why not?
2. Is it ever OK to lie? If yes, in what situations?

Modern Art

Before You Read

Answer the following questions.

1. What kind of art do you like most? Are there any artists you particularly like or dislike?

_____

_____

2. What art galleries are famous in your country? Have you been to them? What was your impression?

_____

_____

3. Look at the photograph. Where do you think it was taken?

_____

_____

Target Vocabulary

Match each word with the best meaning.

1. _____ controversial
2. _____ disappointed
3. _____ generate
4. _____ grab
5. _____ messy
6. _____ owe
7. _____ provoke
8. _____ reveal
9. _____ specialize
10. _____ vision

a. feeling that something wasn't as good as you had hoped
b. to need to pay something to someone
c. causing disagreement
d. produce; create
e. an image or hope of what something is or will be like
f. make people aware of something
g. to make angry; to cause a reaction
h. take quickly and roughly
i. untidy
j. study or work in a specific subject area

If you are a modern art lover, you should be sure to drop by the Saatchi Gallery during your visit to London. The original gallery was opened by Charles Saatchi, a British art collector famous for founding the Saatchi and Saatchi advertising agency with his brother. It moved from its old location in St. John's Wood to its new home
5 in County Hall near the Thames[1] in the spring of 2003.

Anyone who has heard reports in the past of the often shocking but always thought-**provoking** works on display at the Saatchi Gallery will not be **disappointed** when visiting the gallery's new location. Along with the exhibits of new British artists on display, the gallery still includes the **controversial** works of Damien Hirst,
10 Tracy Emin, and the Chapman brothers in its permanent collection.

Of the artworks one can see in the Saatchi Gallery, Hirst's works are probably the most well-known. They have certainly **generated** the most publicity for the gallery. Hirst's work first made headlines in the early 1990s when he created art from dead animals. His most notorious works include a seventeen-foot-long tiger shark
15 floating in a tank of formaldehyde[2] and *Away from the Flock*,[3] a lamb in a similar smaller tank, both of which are still on display at the Saatchi Gallery. These tanks of art are called vitrines, which is the name of the glass case used to make them.

Along with Hirst, the Chapman brothers, Dinos and Jake, also **owe** a certain amount of their fame to the Saatchi Gallery. It was through Saatchi that these two
20 brothers came to public attention. On display at the gallery, visitors can see the brothers' **vision** of Hell, made from 30,000 plastic toy soldiers.

Another artist featured at the gallery who has **grabbed** headlines with her art is Tracy Emin. In 1998, Emin provoked controversy when she sold her **messy**, unmade bed[4] to Saatchi as a work of art titled *My Bed*. The work was no steal at £150,000.

25 The Saatchi Gallery doesn't just feature British artists. Another artist displayed in the Saatchi Gallery, whose work is perhaps not quite as over the top as some of the other artists, is Japanese photographer Hiroshi Sugimoto. Sugimoto, who has spent most of his career living in the United States, **specializes** in photographs of famous people from history, taken from wax sculptures of them, and photos of famous
30 buildings.

Are any of these works really art? That is a question you will have to answer for yourself when you visit the Saatchi Gallery. Charles Saatchi himself says, "I don't have any ground rules[5] for judging art. Sometimes you look and don't feel very comfortable with it—but that doesn't tell you very much. It doesn't necessarily
35 **reveal** much about the quality of the work."

The Saatchi Gallery is open Sunday – Thursday 10:00 A.M. – 6:00 P.M., and Friday – Saturday 10:00 A.M. – 10:00 P.M. Admission for adults is £8.50.

_____ **minutes** _____ **seconds** (486 words)

---

[1] **the Thames** a river that passes through London
[2] **formaldehyde** a liquid chemical used to store dead animals
[3] **flock** a group of sheep (or birds)
[4] **unmade bed** untidy, with the sheets not straight
[5] **ground rules** a set of rules for a particular situation

Reading Comprehension

Circle the letter of the best answer.

1. What is the passage mainly about?

    a. how the gallery is designed

    b. the history of the gallery

    c. why Saatchi prefers modern art

    d. the most important works on display in the gallery

2. Which is probably NOT true about the works on display in the gallery?

    a. They are very valuable.

    b. They are quite traditional.

    c. They provoke strong reactions.

    d. They encourage people to think about the nature of art.

3. What is unusual about Hirst's art?

    a. He only paints dead animals.

    b. He uses real animals.

    c. His paintings look very real.

    d. He uses glass to create sculptures of animals.

4. Why is Emin's work, *My Bed,* so special?

    a. She sleeps in the gallery.

    b. It is a very unusual bed.

    c. It was very expensive.

    d. It contains a dead animal.

5. What does the writer imply about Sugimoto's photographs?

    a. They are famous around the world.

    b. They are not as unconventional as other works in the gallery.

    c. They show things that may frighten children.

    d. They were taken long ago, but are only now becoming well-known.

Idioms

Find each idiom in the story.

1. **a steal**—*very cheap; a bargain*
    - This shirt was only five dollars. It was **a steal**.
    - The computer was **a steal** because it is an older model.

2. **over the top**—*too much; too extreme*
    - I didn't like his acting. It was too **over the top**.
    - She made everyone in the class laugh with her **over the top** answers.

3. **drop by**—*stop for a short visit*
    - You're always welcome at our house. **Drop by** any time.
    - She **dropped by** her friend's house on the way home from work.

Vocabulary Reinforcement

A. Circle the letter of the word or phrase that best completes the sentence.

1. I was _____ when the rain stopped our picnic.

   a. jealous   **b.** suspended   **c.** disappointed   **d.** defended

2. Nostrodamus was a fortune-teller who was famous for his _____ of the future.

   a. grabs   **b.** visions   **c.** controversy   **d.** genius

3. At a price of only two hundred dollars, the airplane ticket was _____.

   a. a steal   **b.** a profit   **c.** over the top   **d.** in advance

4. If I'm free this weekend, I'll _____ and see you.

   a. die out   **b.** track down   **c.** give way   **d.** drop by

5. The security guard _____ the thief to stop him from getting away.

   a. revealed   **b.** specialized   **c.** grabbed   **d.** disappointed

6. I hate it when people _____ the end of a movie before I've seen it.

   a. provoke   **b.** put up   **c.** reveal   **d.** owe

7. This bookshop is very _____. It only sells books about Russian history.

   a. specialized   **b.** species   **c.** general   **d.** generating

8. Let me know how much I _____ you, and I'll give you the money tomorrow.

   a. grab   **b.** owe   **c.** stole   **d.** fraud

B. Complete the passage with items from the box. One item is extra.

owes   controversy   generated   messy   disappointed   over the top   provoked

Any traveler who is a fan of modern art will want to drop by the very successful Saatchi
Gallery while visiting London. The gallery (1)_____ a lot of its popularity to the
(2)_____ that its works have (3)_____ in recent years. Among the
works on display there, visitors can see Hirst's dead animals in large glass tanks, and Emin's
(4)_____, unmade bed, which she sold to the gallery for £150,000. These works
have (5)_____ a lot of debate on what art actually is. Some people might think
these works are (6)_____ and maybe not even art, but they certainly make
viewers think and react.

What Do You Think?

  1. Would you like to visit this gallery? Which of the works mentioned would you most
     (and least) like to see?

  2. Do you think that the works described in this passage are "art"? Why or why not?

Review 16-20

A. Circle the correct answer for each question.

1. What does sugar do in water?   **a.** evaporate   **b.** dissolve
2. Which topic might provoke controversy?   **a.** cheap food   **b.** gun control
3. Which can you slide down?   **a.** a pole   **b.** a sword
4. A dramatic event is _____.   **a.** surprising   **b.** not surprising
5. In which room are you more likely to find tiles?   **a.** kitchen   **b.** bedroom
6. When choosing a hotel, which is more important?   **a.** the chandeliers   **b.** the facilities
7. Expensive glasses are sometimes made from _____.   **a.** crystal   **b.** ethics
8. Why might you be suspended from school?   **a.** fighting   **b.** passing all exams
9. How might you feel if you lose a match?   **a.** messy   **b.** disappointed
10. For complaints you should speak to the person _____.   **a.** in charge   **b.** in advance

B. Complete the paragraph with items from the box. Two items are extra.

available	died out	geniuses	impersonating	indicate	knowledge
motive	pretend	sets them apart	specializing	sword	the authorities

Today, for most people, studying martial arts is a sport, rather than a job, but this hasn't always been the case. Perhaps the most famous martial arts experts in history were the ninjas of Japan. Ninjas have been featured in so many TV shows and movies that it is hard to know what is legend and what is true.

One of the main things which (1)_____ from other martial artists is that rather than (2)_____ in one technique, the ninjas were experts at many things. For example, apart from their main weapon, the (3)_____, they also had great (4)_____ of many other kinds of weapons. And, if they found themselves without a weapon, they could use whatever they found (5)_____.

Ninja warriors were also (6)_____ at (7)_____ other people. They would disguise themselves as other people and (8)_____ to be harmless in order to gain access to secrets. This ability made them useful for (9)_____, who would use them as spies. Even though ninjas have almost entirely (10)_____ today, they are as popular as ever. There is even a ninja museum in Japan that attracts visitors from around the world.

C. Circle the odd one out in each group.

1. **a.** decorate   **b.** ruin   **c.** renovate   **d.** repair

2. **a.** landmark   **b.** monument   **c.** tile   **d.** tomb

3. **a.** give up   **b.** catch up   **c.** find out   **d.** track down

4. **a.** driver   **b.** passenger   **c.** pilot   **d.** warrior

5. **a.** indicate   **b.** defend   **c.** reveal   **d.** show

6. **a.** knowledge   **b.** information   **c.** intelligence   **d.** crystal

7. **a.** indicate   **b.** interpret   **c.** decode   **d.** translate

8. **a.** generate   **b.** create   **c.** provoke   **d.** owe

9. **a.** in advance   **b.** as of   **c.** until   **d.** before

10. **a.** warrior   **b.** schedule   **c.** combat   **d.** sword

D. Use the clues below to complete the crossword.

Across

2. I am on vacation _____ five o'clock today. (2 words)
5. The Taj Mahal is actually a very large _____.
7. Many doctors go on to _____ in one area of medicine.
9. _____ that man! He has my wallet.
11. the study of what is right and wrong
13. Thomas Edison, the inventor, was a _____.
14. like a banana
16. The sick lamb was _____ from the rest of the flock. (2 words)
17. There's no one living in that _____ building.

10. This medicine is not _____ in supermarkets.
12. The fortune-teller uses a _____ ball.
14. Her grandfather was killed in _____ during the war.
15. If you are attacked, it is OK to _____ yourself.

Down

1. Before taking this medicine, _____ it in water first.
2. Five hundred dollars for a new car! Wow, what _____! (2 words)
3. I couldn't understand the message. It was in a kind of _____.
4. The builder put new _____ on the bathroom floor.
6. Some _____ people use dogs to help them see.
8. A red light _____ that you should stop.
9. Over time, simple things ___ more complicated things. (3 words)

World Map

Countries ● and places ○ mentioned in the readings:

Europe
1. Belgium
2. England
3. *London*
4. *Thames River*
5. France
6. *Paris*
7. Germany
8. Greece
9. Italy
10. *Rome*
11. Luxembourg
12. Norway
13. Russia
14. *Scotland*
15. *Sealand*
16. Spain

Africa
17. Egypt
18. *Cairo*
19. *Nile River*

Asia/Australasia
20. Australia
21. *Melbourne*
22. *Sydney*
23. China
24. India
25. Iran
26. Iraq
27. *Baghdad*
28. Japan
29. *Minamata Bay, Kyushu*
30. *Tokyo*
31. Korea, Republic of
32. Kuwait
33. Mongolia
34. Philippines
35. Saudi Arabia
36. Singapore
37. Western Samoa

North America
38. Canada
39. *Montreal*
40. Cuba
41. Dominican Republic
42. Mexico
43. *Guadalajara*
44. Puerto Rico
45. United States of America
46. *Alaska*
47. *Bligh Reef, Alaska*
48. *Boston*
49. *California*
50. *Los Angeles*
51. *Milwaukee*
52. *New York*
53. *San Francisco*
54. *San Jose*
55. *Topeka, Kansas*
56. *White Sands National Monument, New Mexico*

South America
57. Venezuela

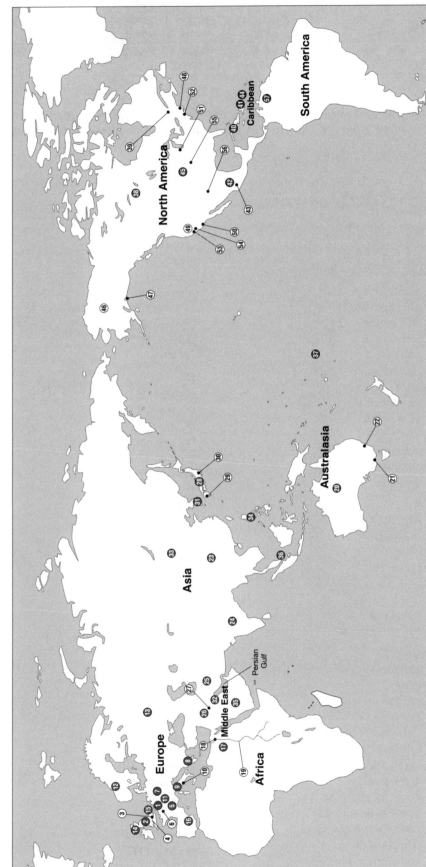

93

Vocabulary Index

Words and phrases included in the Target Vocabulary and Idioms sections are listed below. The number refers to the Unit in which the word or phrase first appears. Idioms are shown in *italics*.

A
abandoned **16**
abnormal **6**
accessible **11**
affect **10**
alien **5**
ally **3**
along with **6**
(to) alternate **18**
archaeologist **2**
architect **6**
artificial **1**
as (the) name suggests **1**
as of (a date or time) **16**
as well as **6**
at fault **10**
attitude **6**
authorities **17**
automatic **8**
available **19**

B
ban **3**
be accustomed to **14**
benefit **1**
blind **18**
boil **15**
brochure **18**
budget **4**
by and large **8**

C
call for **15**
cane **2**
cash in on **12**
catch up (with/to someone) **5**
circumstances **8**
clockwise **5**
code **19**
combat **17**
come as a surprise **14**
come to an end **11**
community **12**
complain **9**
conference **3**

confuse **13**
consist of **5**
contract **14**
controversial **20**
conventional **12**
count **14**
crawl **2**
*a cross between
  (something and something)* **15**
crystal **18**
curved **16**
cycle **5**

D
damage **6**
decorate **13**
defend **17**
(to) design **6**
die out **17**
disappointed **20**
disaster **10**
disgusting **15**
dissolve **18**
diversity **14**
dot **5**
dramatic **19**
drop by **20**

E
empire **11**
enable **3**
entertainer **7**
entire **15**
environment **1**
episode **12**
essential **10**
establish **11**
ethics **17**
evaporate **18**
exchange **12**
expect **4**

F
to face **14**
facilities **16**
factor **8**

feast **15**
find (something + adjective) **3**
float **10**
flow **12**
fraud **19**
fry **15**
fund **1**

G
generate **20**
genius **19**
gesture **8**
get lost **13**
give way to **17**
give/take advice **13**
go all out **15**
go on **13**
(just) go to show **14**
go with **7**
grab **20**
grief **13**

H
harm **10**
haunt **13**
*have (something/nothing)
  to do with* **8**
heir **13**
hold back **7**
holy **11**
honor **5**
humble **4**

I
impersonate **19**
imply **8**
impression **12**
in advance **16**
in charge of **19**
in favor of **16**
in touch (with) **11**
incident **3**
indicate **17**
inject **9**
insane **13**
insect **15**

Author's Acknowledgments

I would like to acknowledge Ki Chul Kang for his inspiration and guidance. I would also like to acknowledge Ji Eun Jung for her honest feedback from the student perspective. Finally, I have to acknowledge all of those students who inspired me to seek out materials to suit the interest of a variety of readers. It was both enjoyable and instructive for me as a teacher and a writer.

I am also grateful to the following teaching professionals who gave very useful feedback as the second edition was being developed.

Casey Malarcher

Andrew White	Induk Institute of Technology, Seoul, South Korea
Chris Campbell	Congress Institute, Osaka, Japan
Claudia Sasía	Instituto México, Puebla, México
Corina Correa	ALUMNI, São Paulo, Brasil
Evelyn Shiang	Tung Nan Institute of Technology, Taipei, Taiwan
Gail Wu	Overseas Chinese Institute of Technology, Taichung, Taiwan
Iain B.M. Lambert	Tokyo Denki University, Tokyo, Japan
Jaeman Choi	Wonkwang University, Chollabukdo, South Korea
Karen Ku	Overseas Chinese Institute of Technology, Taichung, Taiwan
Lex Kim	Lex Kim English School, Seoul, South Korea
Lucila Sotomayor	Instituto D'Amicis, Puebla, México
Marlene Tavares de Almeida	WordShop, Belo Horizonte, Brasil
Pai Sung-Yeon	Charlie's International School, Seoul, South Korea
Pauline Kao	Tung Nan Institute of Technology, Taipei, Taiwan
Richmond Stroupe	World Language Center, Soka University, Tokyo, Japan
Robert McLeod	Kang's Language School, Seoul, South Korea
Sherri Lynn Leibert	Congress Institute, Tokyo, Japan
Shwu Hui Tsai	Chung Kuo Institute of Technology, Taipei, Taiwan
Taming Hsiung	Chung Kuo Institute of Technology, Taipei, Taiwan